my

Understanding

Macbeth

Understanding

Macbeth

New and future titles in the Understanding Great Literature series include:

Understanding

Macbeth

UNDERSTANDING GREAT LITERATURE

Thomas Thrasher

Lucent Books
10911 Technology Place
San Diego, CA 92127

Cover: "Lady Macbeth Seizing the Daggers" by Henry Fuseli

Library of Congress Cataloging-in-Publication Data

Thrasher, Thomas, 1968–
    Macbeth / by Thomas E. Thrasher.
        p. cm. — (Understanding great literature)
    Includes bibliographical references and index.
    ISBN 1-56006-998-8 (hardback: alk. paper)
    1. Shakespeare, William, 1564–1616. Macbeth—Juvenile literature.
    2. Macbeth, King of Scotland, 11th cent.—In literature—Juvenile
    literature. 3. Tragedy—Juvenile literature. [1. Shakespeare, William,
    1564–1616. Macbeth. 2. Theater—England—History—17th
    century.] I. Title. II. Series.
    PR2823 .T47 2002
    822.3'3—dc21

2001003192

Printed in the U.S.A.

Contents

FOREWORD

"**E**xcept for a living man, there is nothing more wonderful than a book!" wrote the widely respected nineteenth-century teacher and writer Charles Kingsley. A book, he continued, "is a message to us from human souls we never saw. And yet these [books] arouse us, terrify us, teach us, comfort us, open our hearts to us as brothers." There are many different kinds of books, of course; and Kingsley was referring mainly to those containing literature—novels, plays, short stories, poems, and so on. In particular, he had in mind those works of literature that were and remain widely popular with readers of all ages and from many walks of life.

Such popularity might be based on one or several factors. On the one hand, a book might be read and studied by people in generation after generation because it is a literary classic, with characters and themes of universal relevance and appeal. Homer's epic poems, the *Iliad* and the *Odyssey*, Chaucer's *Canterbury Tales*, Shakespeare's *Hamlet* and *Romeo and Juliet*, and Dickens's *A Christmas Carol* fall into this category. Some popular books, on the other hand, are more controversial. Mark Twain's *Huckleberry Finn* and J. D. Salinger's *The Catcher in the Rye*, for instance, have their legions of devoted fans who see them as great literature; while others view them as less than worthy because of their racial depictions, profanity, or other factors.

Still another category of popular literature includes realistic modern fiction, including novels such as Robert Cormier's *I Am the Cheese* and S. E. Hinton's *The Outsiders*. Their keen social insights and sharp character portrayals have consistently reached out to and captured the imaginations of many teenagers and young adults; and for this reason they are often assigned and studied in schools.

These and other similar works have become the "old standards" of the literary scene. They are the ones that people most often read, discuss, and study; and each has, by virtue of its content, critical success, or just plain longevity, earned the right to be the subject of a book examining its content. (Some, of course, like the *Iliad* and *Hamlet*, have been the subjects of numerous books already; but their literary stature is so lofty that there can never be too many books about them!) For millions of readers and students in one generation after another, each of these works becomes, in a sense, an adventure in appreciation, enjoyment, and learning.

The main purpose of Lucent's Understanding Great Literature series is to aid the reader in that ongoing literary adventure. Each volume in the series focuses on a single literary work that a majority of critics and teachers view as a classic and/or that is widely studied and discussed in schools. A typical volume first tells why the work in question is important. Then follow detailed overviews of the author's life, the work's historical background, its plot, its characters, and its themes. Numerous quotes from the work, as well as by critics and other experts, are interspersed throughout and carefully documented with footnotes for those who wish to pursue further research. Also included is a list of ideas for essays and other student projects relating to the work, an appendix of literary criticisms and analyses by noted scholars, and a comprehensive annotated bibliography.

The great nineteenth-century American poet Henry David Thoreau once quipped: "Read the best books first, or you may not have a chance to read them at all." For those who are reading or about to read the "best books" in the literary canon, the comprehensive, thorough, and thoughtful volumes of the Understanding Great Literature series are indispensable guides and sources of enrichment.

The Darkest Tragedy

It has been said that only time can judge art—that is, good art will continue to be relevant and remembered long after its creator has vanished. This is the case with Dante's *Inferno*, Mozart's *Eine kleine Nachtmusik*, and Leonardo da Vinci's *Mona Lisa*. The same case can be made for William Shakespeare's *The Tragedy of Macbeth*.

Shakespeare penned *Macbeth* some time between 1604 and 1606, yet the play continues to be as relevant today as it was when he first composed it almost four hundred years ago. Centuries of audiences and readers have been enthralled by Macbeth's escalating outrages as he, spurred by an uncontrollable ambition, achieves his goals through the cold-blooded murder of his king and cousin, his friend, and his enemy's wife and children. Modern audiences are drawn to the play because of its portrayal of brutal ambition, a trait that is still relevant in today's world, and by its psychologically accurate representation of a guilty subconscious forcing its way to the surface.

Nevertheless, *Macbeth* has not been without debate. Although some scholars have hailed the play as Shakespeare's ultimate tragic masterpiece, others have condemned the play as an abridgement of a longer Shakespeare work by an unknown person. Also, scholars cannot agree on many aspects of *Macbeth*: How much control do the Weird Sisters have over Macbeth? Is *Macbeth* truly a tragedy? How much blame does Lady Macbeth deserve for the crimes her husband commits?

Despite the arguments of critics, audiences and readers continue to enjoy *Macbeth*. What is it about this play that makes it a persistent favorite? It has plenty of action and catastrophe, but it lacks comedy and romance. Its hero is largely unsympathetic, and audiences can hardly wait for Macbeth's downfall. In fact, it could be said that *Macbeth* lacks anything that might recommend itself to audiences. Yet it has been read, performed, and studied for almost four hundred years. The reason Shakespeare's *The Tragedy of Macbeth* continues to be relevant today is because it offers an unflinching glimpse into the dark soul of men everywhere.

CHAPTER ONE

The Life of William Shakespeare

W illiam Shakespeare's father, John, was a man of humble origins. The son of a tenant farmer from the village of Snitterfield, he left home to take up an apprenticeship as a glove maker in the nearby town of Stratford-upon-Avon. Little did John Shakespeare know that this action would link his surname with that of Stratford, the town that would forever be known as the birthplace of the greatest writer in the English language.

After John Shakespeare finished his apprenticeship (a term of about seven years), he established his own shop in Stratford and began making gloves and leather goods for the local gentry. He must have done well because there are records of him purchasing land and houses in the surrounding area. As a matter of fact, John Shakespeare first appears in local records on April 29, 1552, when he was fined for keeping a dunghill on a corner of his newly acquired property on Henley Street.

When Stratford-upon-Avon received its charter of incorporation from the Crown in 1553, it allowed the town to elect a common council of burgesses and aldermen to manage local affairs. John Shakespeare, in addition to running a thriving business, also began to take a hand in running the town's affairs. In 1556 he was elected ale taster, a duty that included making sure that bakers made full-weight loaves of bread and that brewers made untainted beer and ale. Two years later, in 1558, John Shakespeare was named a constable (a type of police officer), and it became his job to preserve the town's peace. Other promotions quickly followed: In 1559 he was named affeeror (an official who decided how much to charge for fines); from 1561 to 1563 he served as a burgess; in 1565 he was elected an alderman; and in 1568 he was chosen to be the bailiff (a position roughly equivalent to a modern mayor). For John Shakespeare, the transformation must have been striking, for a man who came into a town a poor apprentice had risen to become one of its most respected citizens.

John Shakespeare married Mary Arden sometime between 1556 and 1558. For John, the marriage would increase his wealth and add a hint of nobility to his otherwise common status. The Ardens, despite a noble heritage, were ordinary folk composed of prosperous farmers and merchants. Mary was the youngest daughter of Robert Arden, and shortly before marrying John, she had

William Shakespeare was born and raised in this house at Stratford-upon-Avon, England.

inherited a good portion of her father's estate. By marrying John, Mary would receive a degree of status (John was a successful merchant and a rising local leader) and a husband who could manage her considerable holdings and provide for their large family.

The Shakespeares had a total of eight children. Mary gave birth to their first daughter, Joan, in 1558. It is unclear what became of Joan, but it is thought that she died while still a baby. The Shakespeares' next child, Margaret, was born in 1562 and died one year later. William Shakespeare was born in 1564. Two years later, William's younger brother Gilbert was born. In 1569 the Shakespeares had another daughter whom they also named Joan. This Joan survived her infancy and lived until 1646. The year 1571 saw the birth of another Shakespeare family member, Anne, who died eight years later. Richard Shakespeare was born in 1574, and the youngest Shakespeare, Edmund, was born in 1580.

The exact date of William Shakespeare's birth is unknown. It is known that he was baptized on April 26, 1564. Tradition holds that he was born on April 23, a reasonable assumption because it was customary for parents to christen their children three days after their birth. Whatever the exact date of William's birth, one thing is clear: He survived his infancy (remarkable considering that the bubonic plague visited Stratford the following summer, killing about one-sixth of the entire population).

Shakespeare's Education

In Elizabethan England, academic education was a privilege. Typically only the children of wealthy parents had the time and opportunity to attend school. Illiteracy was commonplace. Neither John nor Mary Shakespeare could write, but they were not alone. During Queen Elizabeth's reign (1533–1603), 70 percent of all men and 90 percent of all women could not sign their names.

In Stratford, however, education was free to the sons of its burgesses (the town's representatives to Parliament) and aldermen (similar to councilmen), of whom John was one. Given that privilege, he and Mary made sure that their son William could not only read but write his name as well. Male students began to attend classes at the age of five, going first to a "petty" school taught by an abecedarius, or usher. These ushers taught their pupils the alphabet and the Lord's Prayer using a horn-book, a piece of paper framed in wood and covered for pro-tection by a thin layer of trans-parent horn. The mark of the cross preceded the alphabet, so it was called the "Christ cross-row." At seven years of age, after learning the basics in petty school, the students were ready for grammar school.

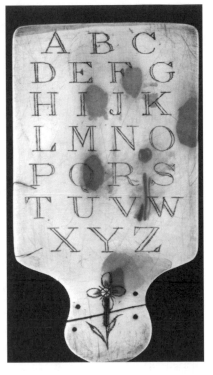

A hornbook, like the one shown here, helped William Shakespeare learn to read and write as a child.

Based on comments scattered throughout his plays, William Shakespeare may not have enjoyed his school years. In *Romeo and Juliet* he writes, "Love goes toward love as schoolboys from their books, / But love from love, toward school with heavy looks."[1] Gremio, a character in *The Taming of the Shrew*, voices Shakespeare's attitude about school when he returns from Petruchio's troublesome wedding and states "as willingly e'er I came from school."[2]

Regardless of how Shakespeare felt about his schooling, it pro-vided him with, as Ben Johnson comments, the "small Latin and less Greek"[3] that he would need to succeed in his later profession. In grammar school Shakespeare studied William Lily's *Short*

15

Introduction of Grammar. The first half of the book laid out the basics of English grammar while the second part contained the rules for Latin. For moral instruction the students would read, in Latin, Erasmus's *Cato*, the fables of Aesop, the *Metamorphoses* of Ovid, and Plutarch's *Lives*. The course of the study also included Greco-Roman playwrights (which introduced young William to classical comedy and the five-act structure of plays), rhetoric (which he used for dramatic effect), logic, and numeration (simple math).

In about 1577 John Shakespeare's fortunes began to decline. In 1578 he mortgaged a house and fifty-six acres (part of his wife's inheritance) to his brother-in-law, Lambert Arden, for a cash loan. John was unable to repay the loan, and this part of his wife's inheritance was forever lost. Later that same year he mortgaged another section of Mary's inheritance, some eighty-six acres, for a set term of years. John's financial troubles continued. Over the next few years he had several fines levied against him by the courts for debts. Tax records of the period make it clear that the one-time alderman's finances were so bad he could not appear in church "for feare of process [arrest] for debbte."[4]

The young William Shakespeare was directly affected by his father's misfortunes. When he was thirteen, his father withdrew him from grammar school. Nicholas Rowe, one of Shakespeare's earliest biographers, writes that the narrowness of his father's "circumstances, and the want of [William's] assistance at home . . . forc'd his father to withdraw him thence."[5] The severance from academia makes some modern scholars doubt whether Shakespeare had enough education to have written the plays credited to him. Although no firm conclusion can be drawn about this, it must be pointed out that he did have a basic education (math, grammar, reading, writing, and Latin). It is also conceivable that Shakespeare continued to educate himself after leaving school, a task made easier because of a burgeoning new business called printing.

Marriage and "the Lost Years"

Some researchers speculate that, after John Shakespeare withdrew his son from Stratford's school, William was placed in a noble

Pictured, is Anne Hathaway's cottage in Shottery, near Stratford-upon-Avon. She married Shakespeare in 1582.

family as a servant. These scholars believe that it was at this point that Shakespeare was exposed to higher learning and the aristocratic society that he would write about later in his life. However plausible this scenario may be, considering his father's financial circumstances, it is more likely that William worked in his father's shop as a glover's apprentice.

In 1582 the glover's apprentice married Anne Hathaway. Like his father, William married a woman of modest social rank. Anne Hathaway came from a family of established yeomen (small farmers who cultivate their own land), and she had inherited a good sum of money from her father after his death. Anne was eight years older than her husband (she was twenty-six and he was eighteen when they married). Shakespeare had not achieved his majority (the age at which a boy legally became a man) and was still considered a minor. Because of his status as a minor, and since the wedding could not be completed before Advent (a religious season during which marriages were normally forbidden), a special license had to be secured from the bishop of Worcester. Once this license had been issued on November 27, 1582, William Shakespeare and Anne Hathaway became husband and wife.

Six months later it became obvious why the odd marriage had taken place. Anne gave birth to a daughter, Susanna, on May 26, 1583. This means that Anne must have been three months pregnant at the time William married her. Two years later, in February 1585, Anne Shakespeare gave birth again, this time to fraternal twins, Hamnet and Judith.

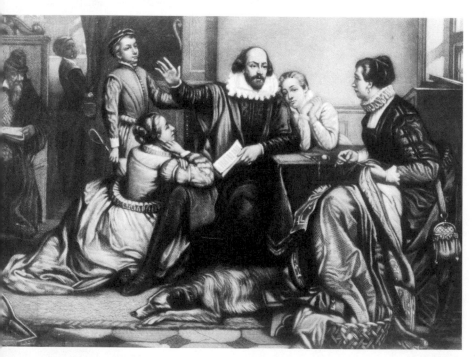

Shakespeare reads to his family. Later in his life, he seemed to regret settling down so young.

William Shakespeare seems to have regretted his early marriage later in his life, and his plays contain many references that seem to criticize his own youthful misadventures. In *A Midsummer Night's Dream*, Lysander tries to talk his way into Hermia's bed, saying, "One turf shall serve as pillow for us both, / One heart, one bed, two bosoms, one troth." Hermia turns him away, telling him to "lie further off, in humane modesty; / Such separation as may well be said / Becomes a virtuous bachelor and a maid."[6] In *Romeo and Juliet* (written at about the same time as *A Midsummer Night's Dream*), Juliet warns against Romeo swearing his love by the moon, saying, "O, swear not by the moon, th' inconstant moon, / That monthly changes in her circled orb, / Lest that thy love prove likewise variable." Juliet then goes on to tell Romeo, "If thy bent of love be honorable, / thy purpose marriage, send some word to-morrow, / By one that I'll procure to come to thee, / Where and what time thou wilt perform the rite."[7] Some critics suggest that the inspiration for *Romeo and Juliet* springs from Shakespeare's hasty marriage to Anne and that the play expresses Shakespeare's disapproval of young love and marriage.

Whatever the case may be for the inspiration of *Romeo and Juliet*, it is generally agreed that William Shakespeare worked as an apprentice in his father's shop until the birth of his twins in 1585. It stands to reason that, faced with a new wife and three hungry mouths to feed, Shakespeare would keep the job he had been employed in since leaving grammar school. However, after 1585 Shakespeare fades from sight until he resurfaces in London in 1592 as the object of a scathing attack by playwright Robert Greene.

Many Shakespeare biographers refer to the period 1585 to 1592 as "the Lost Years." Because of the lack of records, speculation and myth have been quick to step in. Most scholars favor the idea that Shakespeare spent the Lost Years apprenticed to an acting company. Although no hard evidence exists to support this, it is not beyond belief that a restless William Shakespeare asked a visiting company for employment and that the company, seeing the young man's intelligence and quick wit, agreed to take him on as a hired man or apprentice actor. For Shakespeare, employment with an acting troupe was a step up the economic ladder: The troupes paid better than any other job available to him. There are as many different opinions on how Shakespeare spent the Lost Years as there are scholars to argue them. Various researchers have asserted that he worked as a teacher, a sailor, a soldier, or a lawyer's assistant or that he traveled in Italy (thereby acquiring a knowledge of Italy and Italian culture that shows up in many of his plays, including *Romeo and Juliet*). One fact is certain, however: He somehow found his way to London.

The Early Years in London

Shakespeare came to London, as Petruchio says in *The Taming of the Shrew*, on "Such wind as scatters young men through the world / to seek their fortunes farther than at home, / where small experience grows."[8] And, indeed, it was in London where William Shakespeare made his fortune. London was a metropolis in more ways than one. It was the home of a thousand entertainments. A person could attend fencing exhibitions, boxing matches (with no gloves), and public executions. For those who favored the violence of animals over the violence of men, there were arenas specializing in bear baiting (a "sport" in which a chained bear fought off a pack of dogs) and cockfights. There were merchants selling everything from apples to yarn, including the latest imports from America and India: tobacco and tea. For people who preferred the sins of the flesh, there were hundreds of taverns and thousands of prostitutes. However, the thing that impressed most travelers to London was not in the city itself but in a field a short distance north of the city walls in an area known as Shoreditch.

It was in Shoreditch that James Burbage, in 1576, built a round three-story building and named it the Theatre. It was the first time that the word *theatre* had been used in English to refer to a public place for plays. The reason Burbage had to establish the Theatre outside of the city limits was because authorities thought of actors as "rogues, vagabonds, and sturdy beggars"[9] who created unrest. Acting troupes had such bad reputations that they had to have the patronage of nobles in order to avoid persecution. To show their appreciation, the acting companies named themselves after their patrons, such as the Queen's Men or the Lord Chamberlain's Men.

It is thought that around 1589 Shakespeare joined, or somehow became associated with, the combined companies of the Lord Strange's Men and the Admiral's Men. Although records exist of his acting, it is unlikely that Shakespeare was a star actor. At twenty-five years of age he was too old to play female roles (since women were forbidden by law from acting, young boys played female roles) and too old to begin an apprenticeship as an actor. It is likely that he got his start in the theater as a hired man, probably as a bookkeeper. Like the modern stage manager, it was the job of the bookkeeper to make sure that things ran smoothly during a performance.

The bookkeeper's most important duty was to keep the company's playbook. Since copyright laws did not exist at the time, each company kept the texts of the plays they performed secret. It was the bookkeeper's responsibility to buy plays, to get the appropriate license from the Revels Office (the government censor), and to revise the plays according to the actors' criticisms, the troupe's needs, and the government's standards. The bookkeeper also had to copy out the parts for the actors. It is perhaps from his experience as a bookkeeper that Shakespeare developed his keen dramatic instinct. And if Shakespeare was indeed a bookkeeper, it is likely that this background, and the added financial opportunity that playwriting offered, led him to compose his own plays. It would allow him to get paid twice: once as a writer and then again as a bookkeeper. Shakespeare the businessman was always on the lookout for extra income.

William Shakespeare's first four history plays (*Henry VI*, Parts 1, 2, and 3, and *Richard III*) made him a force to be reckoned with on the Elizabethan stage. Shakespeare was capitalizing on public opinion. Written between 1589 and 1593, his tetralogy is a celebration of national pride. In 1588 the Spanish Armada had been defeated by Britain despite overwhelming odds. Patriotism in England was at a high, and audiences were thrilled to see the history of their country acted out on stage.

Shakespeare's theatrical success did not escape the notice of his rival playwrights. Some of the playwrights were enthusiastic about the history plays, but others were not. Rival playwright Robert Greene called Shakespeare "an upstart crow, beautified with our feathers, that with his Tygers heart wrapt in a Player's hide, supposes he is as well able to bombast out a blank verse as the rest of you: and being an absolute Johannes Factotum [a jack-of-all-trades], is in his own conceit the only Shake-scene in a country." Greene's anger arose from his belief that Shakespeare, since he lacked a university education, was an inferior writer compared to Greene and his fellow University wits. Greene believed that university-educated writers were better than "those puppets [actors] . . . that spake from our mouths"[10] and was upset that an outsider like Shakespeare, who was not only undereducated but an actor as well, was being praised by both the nobility and the masses.

Greene's attack had little effect on Shakespeare's growing popularity. Shakespeare began to write plays at the rate of about two a year. Following the success of his historical tetralogy, Shakespeare expanded his creative horizons beyond dramatizing his country's history. During this period he wrote *Titus Andronicus* and *The Comedy of Errors*, his first tragedy and his first comedy.

The Plague Years: 1592–1594

Both *Titus Andronicus* and *The Comedy of Errors* were well received by the public, and things were going smoothly for the budding playwright when disaster struck. Between 1592 and 1594, the plague ravished London, killing almost eleven thousand people. To combat the plague, people were kept out of confined areas that facilitated the spread of the disease; thus, the

The Elizabethan dramatist Robert Greene, crudely depicted in this woodcut, resented Shakespeare for not having a university education.

public theaters were closed by royal decree. The closing of the theaters put Shakespeare out of work, and he was forced to earn a living by different means.

In 1593, during the worst of the plague, Shakespeare published his first book. The slim volume contained the poem "Venus and Adonis," an erotic narrative written in the style of Shakespeare's rival Christopher Marlowe. The book was enormously popular, and one biographer noted that "Multitudes bought 'Venus and Adonis'; the poem went through sixteen editions before 1640. No other work by Shakespeare achieved so many printings during this period. Readers thumbed it until it fell to pieces." [11] The sequel to "Venus and Adonis" was published the following year in 1594. Although it never attained the popularity of "Venus and Adonis," "The Rape of Lucrece" nonetheless went on to be reprinted several times before 1640. Although both "Venus and Adonis" and "The Rape of Lucrece" are today considered inferior to his plays, the two poems tell us something about the man writing them. During this period of his life, with the public theaters closed, William Shakespeare tried to make a living by writing poetry calculated to appeal to a select audience: university students, courtiers, lawyers, and, above all, the nobility.

"Venus and Adonis" and "The Rape of Lucrece" were both dedicated to the nineteen-year-old earl of Southampton, Henry Wriothesley. The reason for the dedication was simple: money. With the public theaters closed because of the plague, Shakespeare was effectively out of work as a playwright. When Shakespeare dedicated his "unpolished lines to your Lordship,"[12] he was hoping to secure patronage from the young earl. The tradition of patronage was a holdover from the medieval era when artists of all kinds (poets, painters, singers, actors) depended on the nobility for their livelihoods. The nobles gave money to the artists in return for performances and works of art.

The relationship between Southampton and Shakespeare is unclear, but it is certain that Southampton provided Shakespeare with some type of financial assistance during the plague years. Nicholas Rowe tells of "one instance so singular in the magnificence of this patron of Shakespeare's . . . that my Lord Southampton, at one time, gave him [Shakespeare] a thousand pounds, to enable him to go through with a purchase which he [Southampton] heard he [Shakespeare] had a mind to."[13] Although the amount here is unrealistic (at the time of his death, Shakespeare's combined holdings were not worth a thousand pounds), there is little doubt that Henry Wriothesley, earl of Southampton, contributed in some way to Shakespeare's livelihood. Scholars believe that Southampton gave Shakespeare the money he needed to buy an interest in the Lord Chamberlain's Men when it re-formed after the plague abated.

At about the same time that Shakespeare wrote and published "Venus and Adonis" and "The Rape of Lucrece," he began work on his famous series of sonnets. Generally, sonnets celebrate the undying love of the poet for his beloved, usually a woman, by listing her beauties and virtues in ornate language. Shakespeare's sonnets are unusual and famous because of their variation on the traditional Italian sonnet rhyme scheme. *Romeo and Juliet* was especially influenced by Shakespeare's work on the sonnets; the play contains several sonnets and seems to embody the fragile world of courtly love. There is little doubt among critics and biographers that *Romeo and Juliet*, as well as several other plays, were composed during the plague years with an eye toward the time when the public theaters would reopen.

The Lord Chamberlain's Men

When the plague that had been ravishing London finally loosened its grip on the city in 1595, Shakespeare went back to work. Members of the upper classes, who had fled the deadly city for the healthy countryside, were returning. Everyone from the humblest apprentice to the greatest lord was starving for entertainment after the horror of the plague.

Shakespeare bought a share (probably with the money from Southampton) in the re-formed Lord Chamberlain's Men and joined his friends Richard Burbage and William Kemp. Shakespeare became the "ordinary poet" for the Lord Chamberlain's Men, which meant that he was the company's playwright. *Professional* is

After the plague was over, Richard Burbage (pictured above) joined Shakespeare in re-forming the acting troupe of Lord Chamberlain's Men.

Shakespeare and the Lord Chamberlain's Men often performed for Queen Elizabeth.

the best word to describe Shakespeare during this period. Only a few writers during Shakespeare's life were as prolific as he was, especially between 1594 and 1595. His plays display the poetic skills he developed during the plague while he was writing sonnets and the poems for Southampton. Shakespeare was beginning to develop the dramatic technique that would reach perfection in his tragedies and romances.

Four of Shakespeare's comedies were produced during this period: *The Taming of the Shrew*, *The Two Gentlemen of Verona*, *Love's Labor's Lost*, and the fanciful *A Midsummer Night's Dream*. At the same time that Shakespeare was exploring the genre of comedy, he was also writing plays that he knew would sell, such as the histories *King John* and *Richard II*. Shakespeare also produced his second tragedy during this period. *Romeo and Juliet* was hugely successful and continues to be one of his most popular plays, after *Hamlet*.

Shakespeare's star was on the rise. He and the Lord Chamberlain's Men first performed for Queen Elizabeth during the yuletide festivities of 1594. With the deaths of two of Shakespeare's rivals, Christopher Marlowe and Thomas Kyd,

Shakespeare and his acting troupe were in constant demand. In 1596 Shakespeare was awarded a coat of arms from the College of Arms. This had been Shakespeare's lifelong dream, and it allowed him to legally sign himself "Gentleman." A gentleman had two primary advantages over a commoner: First, it confirmed class status as a member of the gentry, and secondly, a gentleman could testify and bring suit in court without taking an oath.

This piece of personal fortune was marred by the death of Shakespeare's only son, Hamnet, who was buried on August 11, 1596. The death of his son ended any hope Shakespeare may have had for continuing the family name. Although Shakespeare's daughter, Susanna, gave birth to his granddaughter, Elizabeth Hall, Elizabeth Hall remained childless throughout her life which is why no direct descendants of William Shakespeare exist today. In more ways than one, 1596 was a pivotal year in Shakespeare's life.

To reinforce his newly acquired status as a gentleman, Shakespeare bought the biggest house in Stratford-upon-Avon in 1597. It is ironic that as Shakespeare was securing for himself the trappings of a country gentleman in Stratford, he failed to pay his taxes in London. This failure to pay taxes has caused a few scholars to wonder about Shakespeare's financial state, and they believe that his resources were stretched to the limit at this time.

However, Shakespeare's success in the theater continued during the 1596–1597 season. He produced two works, which coincidently contain his two most memorable characters. The first was the comedy *The Merchant of Venice*, which contains the character Shylock. The second play was a history called *Henry IV*, which contains the character Falstaff. *Henry IV* was such a huge success that it spawned three sequels: *Henry IV, Part 2; Henry V;* and the comedy *The Merry Wives of Windsor*. Scholars believe that *The Merry Wives of Windsor* was written at the command of Queen Elizabeth, who ordered the performance be given in front of her and her court during the Garter Feast on St. George's Day, April 23, 1597 (Shakespeare's thirty-third birthday).

Shakespeare and the Globe

In 1598 William Shakespeare could easily call himself England's most popular playwright. The unparalleled box-office success of his history plays, most notably *Henry IV*, Parts 1 and Part 2, had earned him the praise that other playwrights only dreamed of. His comedies and tragedies were acclaimed by everyone from Queen Elizabeth down to the humblest apprentice with a penny and an afternoon to spare. This sense of achievement was underscored by Francis Meres, who praised Shakespeare extensively in his book *Palladis Tamia* and compared him to the Greco-Roman playwrights.

The year 1598 came to a dramatic end when the longtime theatrical home of Shakespeare and the Lord Chamberlain's Men, the Theatre, was torn down. Under the cover of darkness, a small group gathered at the empty Theatre. The group dismantled the playhouse and carried the timbers through London, then ferried them across the Thames River to Bankside, a district just outside the southern city limits. There, the group reassembled the theater and renamed it the Globe.

The Globe saw the production of some of Shakespeare's best-known plays. It was the first place that the comedies *Much Ado About Nothing, As You Like It, Twelfth Night,* and *All's Well That Ends Well* were first performed. It was also the place that saw the inaugural performances of *Julius Caesar* and *Hamlet. Hamlet* is the play that marks the beginning of Shakespeare's great tragedies. It is by far the most recognized of his plays.

Despite a string of hits, a growing personal fortune, and an increasing recognition of his talent as a playwright, William Shakespeare's life at this point was replete with troubles. His father, John, died in September 1601. Whatever personal grief this may have caused Shakespeare, it paled in comparison to the grief caused by a performance of *Richard II* in February 1601. A group of rebellious nobles (including Shakespeare's friend and patron, the earl of Southampton) attempted to overthrow Queen Elizabeth. As part of their plan, they paid the Lord Chamberlain's

Men to perform *Richard II* in the hope that the play would influence the populace of London to support their cause. The ploy and the rebellion were complete failures. The rebels were captured by the queen's forces and were quickly executed. A few of the rebels, including the earl of Southampton, escaped the hangman's noose and were confined to the Tower of London for the rest of Queen Elizabeth's reign. The investigation after the rebellion cleared the Lord Chamberlain's Men of any intentional wrongdoing. Shakespeare and his fellows breathed a sigh of relief after being cleared by the queen; if they had been found guilty, their playhouse would have been torn down, their fortunes would have been ruined, and they would have been executed.

The King's Men

The Elizabethan era came to an end on March 24, 1603, when Queen Elizabeth died at the age of seventy. Just before she died,

The Globe theater premiered some of Shakespeare's best-known plays.

29

she called her ministers to her and named her successor: "I will that a king succeed me, and who but my kinsman the King of Scots."[14] When James VI of Scotland arrived in London, the reception was muted. The plague was once again ravaging the city (30,561 deaths in one year), and those who could flee the city had already done so. Nonetheless, James VI assumed the throne of England as King James I.

As during previous visitations of the plague, the public theaters were closed, but that did not stop James I from indulging his interest in drama. Within ten days of his arrival in London, he ordered his ministers to issue a royal warrant to the Lord Chamberlain's Men that made the acting company the servant of the king. The troupe, out of respect for its new patron, changed the name of the company to the King's Men. The royal warrant proves that Shakespeare and the King's Men were the most important acting troupe in existence at that time.

A portrait of William Shakespeare.

During the reign of James I, acting was not only endorsed as a legitimate profession for Shakespeare and his fellow actors, but it was profitable as well. Under James, the rate of pay for court performances was raised from the ten pounds Queen Elizabeth had paid to twenty pounds a performance. In addition, the number of performances at court doubled because both King James and his wife, Queen Anne, were fascinated by English drama. They wanted to see all of the plays they had missed while living in Scotland. Shakespeare and his company were happy to oblige and performed more times at court than all of the other London troupes combined. Money flowed into the company's coffers. This was the most profitable time the acting profession had yet to enjoy.

Between 1603 and 1607, Shakespeare wrote some of his best work. He wrote the comedy *Measure for Measure* to appeal to the new king's interests: justice and mercy. These years also saw the production of Shakespeare's finest tragedies: *Othello, King Lear, Macbeth,* and *Antony and Cleopatra.* Like *Measure for Measure, Macbeth* was calculated to appeal to King James's other interests: demonology and treachery. *Coriolanus* and *Timon of Athens* followed Shakespeare's greatest tragedies, and although these plays are technically good, they demonstrate a growing dissatisfaction with the genre of tragedy. In these plays, Shakespeare seems to be groping for something more, something beyond both comedy and tragedy.

In 1608 Shakespeare became a shareholder in the Blackfriars Theatre. The Blackfriars was an intimate theater, seating only three hundred people compared to the three thousand that might squeeze into the Globe on any given day. Because seating was limited, ticket prices were higher and the audience was a little more select and sophisticated than the average Globe audience. The success of the Blackfriars Theatre was partly due to the plays that Shakespeare wrote for this new select audience.

Shakespeare wrote neither tragedies, comedies, nor histories but rather a curious blend of all three genres, called romances. The romances were often Greek stories of love and overwhelming experiences such as quests or shipwrecks. Shakespeare's romances *Pericles* and *Cymbeline* were renowned for their special effects, such as gods descending from the heavens. These spectacles further increased Shakespeare's celebrity status, and his works, including his sonnets, were openly pirated and sold by booksellers.

Shakespeare's good fortune was not restricted to his professional life; it was rolling over into his private life as well. Shakespeare's oldest daughter, Susanna, married Dr. John Hall in 1607. A year after the marriage, Shakespeare's first grandchild, Elizabeth Hall, was born. However, later that same year

Shakespeare's mother, Mary, died, and she was buried next to her husband in the churchyard at Stratford-upon-Avon.

Back to Stratford

In 1608 or 1609 Shakespeare moved back to Stratford and became a permanent resident who made infrequent trips to London to see to his theater business and to produce an occasional play. Shakespeare was settling into the role he had been practicing for all of his life: the successful country gentleman. After turning his back on the city that had made him famous and wealthy, Shakespeare began to take a more active interest in the affairs of his hometown.

Shakespeare was involved in several lawsuits concerning the use of land in the vicinity of Stratford, and he made at least one trip to London for the express purpose of petitioning the Crown to fix the roads between Stratford and London. He was also called to testify in a nasty civil suit concerning an arranged marriage. Shakespeare's testimony in the suit was of little help to either side, and the matter was referred for arbitration.

Shakespeare also kept busy in his semiretirement by writing plays. The period 1610 to 1613 saw the production of three additional romances (*The Winter's Tale, The Tempest,* and *The Two Noble Kinsmen*) and one history (*Henry VIII*). After the production of *The Noble Kinsmen* in 1613, Shakespeare went into full retirement. He may have returned to London on occasion to collect profits from the Globe and the Blackfriars Theatre, but this is speculation. Nothing in known for sure about Shakespeare until 1616.

On February 12, 1616, William Shakespeare's youngest daughter, Judith, married Thomas Quiney. The marriage was unusual because the groom, a twenty-seven-year-old vintner with a reputation for shadiness, was marrying the thirty-one-year-old daughter of the most famous and richest man in town. Soon after the marriage, a scandal ensued. Quiney was summoned to court to answer charges of fornication and fathering a child outside of wedlock. What began in February as a joyous time in Shakespeare's life turned to embarrassment that spring, then to illness, and then, finally, to death.

The circumstances surrounding Shakespeare's month-long illness and eventual death are unclear. Perhaps it was the stress of the scandal of his daughter's marriage and the subsequent court case brought against his son-in-law, or perhaps it was the result of a drinking party. Whatever the cause, William Shakespeare died on April 23, 1616, appropriately enough, the playwright's fifty-second birthday.

The story of William Shakespeare does not end with his death but begins. During his life, Shakespeare published only three poems. However, in 1623, seven years after his death, the first collection of Shakespeare's plays appeared in print. The collection, called the First Folio, was immensely popular and was reprinted four times by 1685. Since that time, Shakespeare's plays have been reprinted thousands of times and have been translated into all of the world's major languages. Shakespeare's impact is still felt today in common words and phrases and in plays, television shows, and movies. Author James Joyce once observed, "After God, only Shakespeare created more."[15]

CHAPTER TWO

The History
of *Macbeth*

L ike a Hollywood movie producer, William Shakespeare was not above taking a real story, adding some flourishes, and putting it on the stage. This is essentially what he did with all of his history plays and a couple of his tragedies because real life often provides the inspiration for all kinds of fiction. Shakespeare was quite familiar with Raphael Holinshed's *Chronicles of England, Scotland, and Ireland,* which had been published in 1577 and was a well-regarded Renaissance history. As a result, at some point it occurred to Shakespeare to make a tragedy out of the murder of an obscure Scottish king by an equally obscure Scottish nobleman named Macbeth. Similar to modern Hollywood movies, *Macbeth* contains a small amount of truth and a lot of creative embellishment by the historians whom Shakespeare copied.

The Historical Macbeth
Shakespeare's principal source for *Macbeth* was Holinshed's *Chronicles.* Shakespeare's *Macbeth* is reasonably similar to the account given in *Chronicles,* but, as scholar Bruce Heydt has observed, "a whole tradition of myth-making . . . had so coloured and embellished the actual events that neither Holinshed's nor Shakespeare's version can be truthfully called historical." [16]

The historical Macbeth was born in Scotland (the exact date of his birth is unknown). He was the eldest son of Finlaech mac Ruadri, moarmaer of Moray, a provincial ruler under the king's authority (a moarmaer was like a modern governor, except he answered to the king). Under the Scottish inheritance system, eldest sons did not necessarily inherit their father's titles. Monarchs and moarmaers appointed their successors from among the chief nobles of the area, and often brothers and cousins grew up hoping to rule in their own right. Needless to say, this system encouraged intense competition for the Scottish crown and other noble titles, and aspirants often resorted to murdering their rivals in order to increase their chances of obtaining power. While Macbeth was young, his father is believed to have been murdered by two ambitious nephews who desired his title. At the time Macbeth was too young to avenge his father's death, but in 1032 records show that one of the murderous cousins and fifty of his followers were burned to death. Shortly thereafter Macbeth took over his father's former title, moarmaer of Moray, and he married his cousin's widow, Gruoch, the woman who eventually became Shakespeare's inspiration for Lady Macbeth.

At about this time Scotland's King Malcolm II was attempting to replace Scotland's old system of inheritance with the newer system of primogeniture, or inheritance by direct descent. Instead of appointing his successor from among the chief nobles of Scotland, King Malcolm II appointed his daughter's son, Duncan. Heydt has perceived, "This decision must have been doubly galling to many Scottish nobles; not only had Malcolm excluded them from the succession, primogeniture's first application yielded a king of very questionable ability."[17] Nonetheless, upon Malcolm's death, Duncan was

Macbeth (depicted here) became Scotland's king after murdering Duncan I.

35

crowned king of Scotland much to the dismay of many of its nobles.

During this period Scotland was constantly at war, threatened from within and without by many enemies, including the Danish, the Norwegians, and the English. The new king of Scotland, Duncan, led his army against Danish invaders. However, after losing a series of battles, he rebuilt his army and attacked Durham in Northumbria, where he was again defeated and "put to a disorderly flight."[18] Shortly after the fiasco in Northumbria, medieval records show that "Duncan, King of the Scots, was killed . . . by Macbeth son of Finlaech."[19] The exact manner of his death or the motive for the murder remains in question. Some scholars argue that Macbeth killed Duncan on the field of battle while others say Duncan's death was the result of skulduggery. Several historians assert that Macbeth killed Duncan for purely selfish motives, but others believe that Macbeth killed Duncan to protect Scotland's security and prestige. Whatever the case, the result was the same: Macbeth became the king of Scotland and reigned successfully for ten years before being defeated in a battle with invading Danes.

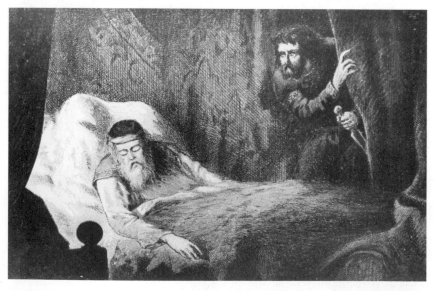

Macbeth murders King Duncan I of Scotland in order to ascend the throne.

Creating the Legend of Macbeth

Although the medieval records are clear about Macbeth, none of the medieval historians mention the Weird Sisters, Banquo, or Lady Macbeth; in all likelihood, they probably did not exist, with the exception of Lady Macbeth. In 1527 Scottish historian Hector Boece added the Weird Sisters, Lady Macbeth, and Banquo to his history of Macbeth in an attempt to strengthen the Stuarts' (the name of the royal family that ruled England and Scotland in Shakespeare's time) claim to the Scottish throne and to discredit their enemies. Boece added the Weird Sisters to suggest that the historical Macbeth gained the Scottish throne through satanic intervention. Boece also bears responsibility for creating Lady Macbeth's sinister reputation. Although Lady Macbeth did exist as Gruoch, there is not enough evidence to establish if she was as cunning as Boece and Shakespeare portray her. Likewise, Banquo was a mythic Scottish figure that Boece "discovered" was the founder of the house of Stuart. Boece included Banquo to make it appear that the Stuarts fulfilled an ancient Scottish prophecy that the descendants of Banquo would inherit the Scottish crown.

When Holinshed was compiling his *Chronicles* for publication in 1577, he merely repeated the faulty findings of Boece. Holinshed's *Chronicles* was the source that Shakespeare used when he was writing *Macbeth*, so he repeated the faulty information that had been supplied to Holinshed. This means that *Macbeth*'s most memorable characters (the Weird Sisters, Lady Macbeth, and Banquo) were not wholly Shakespeare's invention but the creation of Hector Boece. However, Shakespeare was quick to realize the dramatic possibilities of the characters and their potential appeal to his patron, James I. The fact that Banquo was the founder of the house of Stuart would appeal to James I because he was a Stuart himself, and the Weird Sisters would appeal to James's overwhelming fascination with demons, demonology, and witchcraft.

The Writing of *Macbeth*

With Holinshed's *Chronicles* as his guide, Shakespeare began to write *The Tragedy of Macbeth*. Like many aspects of Shakespeare's life, the exact circumstances surrounding the writing of *Macbeth* are unknown. However, scholars suspect that *Macbeth* was written some time between 1604 and 1606 because of various allusions within the play to contemporary events in England. One of the events was the Gunpowder Plot of 1605, which was followed by sensational trials and much public discussion of the Jesuit practice of "equivocation." The third was a public concern, and a royal interest, in witchcraft.

The Gunpowder Plot influenced *Macbeth* in terms of its subject matter—the overthrow of a righteous king by nefarious means—and its theme—the evilness of equivocation. On November 5, 1605, England was shaken by the news that an attempt had been made on the life of James I, the prince, and the entire government of England. The Gunpowder Plot was a plan conceived and executed by a group of Catholic conspirators to assassinate King James and the members of Parliament in the hope of establishing a Catholic government. Throughout the late summer and early fall, the group smuggled barrels of gunpowder and bars of iron (for shrapnel) into a cellar beneath Parliament with the intention of igniting it on November 5, 1605, when James I was supposed to address the entire Parliament. However, the plan was foiled when the king's security forces intercepted a letter from one of the conspirators to a friend in Parliament warning the friend to stay away during the king's November 5 address. The conspirators were caught, imprisoned, and later executed. The English public was shocked that an attempt had been made on the life of their king and government by Catholic conspirators. This caused an anti-Catholic backlash that resulted in the persecution of Catholics in England for centuries.

During the investigation Father Henry Garnet, a Catholic priest of the Jesuit order, was brought to trial as a conspirator because his *A Treatise on Equivocation* was found in the possession of one of the conspirators. This treatise outlined the Jesuit practice of equivocation, or answering questions in a way that would allow for multiple interpretations. The Jesuits developed this practice so

The Gunpowder Plot was an attempt by a group of Catholic conspirators to assassinate King James I.

that they could "honestly" answer questions about things they had learned via the sacrament of confession. This idea influenced Shakespeare when he was writing *Macbeth*, and he made equivocation a central theme of his play. For example, the Weird Sisters tell Macbeth that he will never be vanquished until "Great Birnan wood to high Dunsinane hill / Shall come."[20] This statement is an equivocation because the listener would be likely to interpret it to mean that it could never happen (how could trees move?), but, in fact, the literal meaning of the phrase could come true (branches from the wood could be moved to the hill).

The years 1604 to 1606 also saw an increased interest in, and persecution of, witches in England. The English public, and James I in particular, began to see demons, devils, and witches everywhere. For the most part the "witches" were unmarried or widowed women who lived alone. The fact that a woman would choose to live alone was considered proof enough of her "marriage" to the devil. Consequently, a revised and more severe law against witchcraft was passed, and the persecution of witches intensified. When Shakespeare was writing *Macbeth*, he may have been trying to capitalize on public sentiment about witches and witchcraft by including the Weird Sisters.

The Influence of James I

In addition to contemporary events, Shakespeare was likely influenced by the desire to flatter his new and generous patron, James I. The years since the death of Queen Elizabeth had been tumultuous for England. Her death came as a blow to many English citizens, and the coronation of James I, a Scot, had caused some consternation among the more conservative nobility. Three assassination attempts left the new king paranoid about the loyalty of his retainers. Upon his ascent to the throne,

King James I and his supporters fend off an assassination attempt.

he took Shakespeare's acting company, the Lord Chamberlain's Men, under his protection and doubled the troupe's payment and the number of performances at court. Thus, Shakespeare may have written *Macbeth* to demonstrate his loyalty to the Stuarts and the English monarchy. He also may have written the play in an attempt to appeal to the king's interests and cement his liberal patronage.

Macbeth contains many details and themes that Shakespeare may have used to appeal to King James I, including using Scotland for the setting and inserting a character that was a legendary ancestor of the Stuarts. King James I was fiercely proud of his Scottish heritage and equally proud that his coronation had united the kingdoms of England and Scotland. The Scottish setting of the play would have appealed to James's sense of Scottish pride in spite of the fact that the Stuarts' reputed Scottish ancestor, Banquo, in fact never existed. The inclusion of Banquo, and the altering of his role from the histories of both Boece and Holinshed (in both works Banquo aids in the murder of Duncan), is an attempt by Shakespeare to curry favor with his patron by portraying the House of Stuart in a flattering light.

Macbeth also centers around a couple of themes that would have been especially interesting to King James I: the assassination of a legitimate king and the downfall of the usurper. Since James I had assumed the throne of England in 1603, there had been three attempts on his life by 1605. The one that had come closest to succeeding was the Gunpowder Plot of 1605, which throughly unnerved James I. The king consoled himself with the thought that the assassination of a king was so contrary to the Chain of Being (a long-established belief that placed the king above all mortals and answerable only to God) that the destruction of the assassin was assured. Shakespeare may have obliged James I by writing a play in which a king is murdered by a usurper, but the usurper never enjoys the fruits of the crown and falls almost as quickly as he rose.

Shakespeare also may have included the supernatural element of *Macbeth* because King James I had a long-standing interest in witchcraft (and in persecuting witches) and had written a well-known book on the subject, *Daemonologie*, in 1599. Shakespeare's inclusion of the Weird Sisters and the scenes of magical invocation (a magical formula used to conjure up spirits), such as act 4, scene 1, would have undoubtedly interested the king. Likewise, James had recently acquired an interest in the Jesuit practice of equivocation. Because the conspirators that were captured during the Gunpowder Plot refused to give direct answers to questions, James saw this as proof of the diabolical origins of Catholicism, and Jesuits in particular. To see a play in which, as Macbeth puts it, demons "palter . . . in a double sense" and "keep the word of the promise to our ear, / And break it to our hope"[21] would have embodied James I's opinion on the wickedness of equivocation.

The Performance of *Macbeth*

Because of the references in the play to equivocation, Father Garnet, and the Gunpowder Plot, the majority of Shakespearean scholars agree that *Macbeth* was first performed in 1606 at the Globe. Going to a see a play in Renaissance England was similar to seeing a play today: How much a person paid determined where that spectator sat. The basic admission of one penny entitled one to stand in the "yard" that surrounded the stage on three sides. Because these people stood on the ground, they were called groundlings. Another penny allowed a person to sit in the first tier of wooden seats (cushions were available for rent at the front door), a third penny provided access to the second tier, and a fourth penny to the third tier. If a person wanted to splurge, he could rent a private box or sit on the stage while the play was in progress.

However, going to see a play was also quite different in Renaissance England. Acting was not a respectable profession, and the theaters ranked just above the bear-baiting dens and brothels. Vendors walked through the audience shouting and selling refreshments during the performance. Prostitutes plied their trade behind the curtains of private boxes. Actors, without the aid of sound amplification, had to shout over the noise to be heard. If the audience did not like the play, they would shout at the actors and throw things (like tomatoes, which were sold for that express purpose).

Acting was strictly a male profession in Renaissance England. Female actors were considered lewd and were forbidden by law from appearing on the stage, so young boys played the female roles. Likewise, "respectable" women did not attend the public theater, but many of them did attend disguised as men. The public theater was also used as a rendezvous for people having extramarital affairs.

It is into this circuslike atmosphere that Shakespeare introduced *Macbeth*. It is impossible to know how a Renaissance audience would have responded to the play. Undoubtedly, they would have cheered during the fight scenes, but would the appearance of the Weird Sisters have frightened them? How would they have reacted to Lady Macbeth's scheming ways?

Macbeth's reputation as a cursed play stems from its initial performance. According to legend, before the play's inaugural performance the actor who was going to play Lady Macbeth dropped dead backstage. Supposedly, William Shakespeare assumed the role of Lady Macbeth at the last minute, but this seems unlikely: Shakespeare would have been too old (and probably too bearded) to pass himself off as a woman. Since that performance, the play has subsequently been blamed for a variety of mishaps: In 1703 it was blamed for a storm that devastated London, in 1865 Abraham Lincoln supposedly was reading from *Macbeth* (his favorite play) five days before his assassination, and in 1937, during a rehearsal of the play, Laurence Olivier was almost killed when a weight crashed to the stage, narrowly missing the famed actor. Some people say that the cursed nature of the play stems from its use of the Weird Sisters and its magical invocations that invite spirits to disrupt the play.

During a rehearsal of Macbeth, *a fallen weight narrowly missed the leading actor, Laurence Olivier.*

Macbeth, although one of Shakespeare's greatest tragedies, has proved to be quite unsuccessful on the stage, and there are very few records of the play being performed. It was probably performed for James I and his brother-in-law Christian IV, king of Denmark, during his visit to England in 1606. Although Simon Forman, a London physician and drama fan, recorded seeing "Mackbeth at the Glob, 1610 [1611?], the 20 of Aprill,"[22] it seems that the play was rarely performed during Shakespeare's life and less after he died. Aside from the superstition among actors that *Macbeth* is cursed, the play (until recently) was technically hard to stage in a convincing manner. This discouraged actors, directors, producers, and theater owners from putting on the play.

Early commentary on *Macbeth* is varied. It is unclear how Shakespeare's audience reacted to the play, but fifty years later the diarist Samuel Pepys declared it "a most excellent play in all respects, but especially in divertisement, though it be a deep tragedy; which is a strange perfection in a tragedy."[23] However, five years later in "On the Dramatic Poetry of the Last Age," John Dryden wrote, "In reading some bombast speeches of Macbeth, which are not to be understood, he (Ben Jonson) used to say that it was horror; and I am much afraid this is so."[24] A few years later Dryden continued his criticism by writing, "I cannot deny his failings . . . in his manner of expression: he often obscures his meaning by his words, and sometimes makes it unintelligible." However, Dryden did admit that he considered Shakespeare to have the "most comprehensive soul"[25] of all the poets. It would seem from the scattered records that *Macbeth*, although a great tragedy, was only warmly received by audiences during Shakespeare's life.

What Was Shakespeare Trying to Achieve?

Although Shakespeare is one of the most criticized writers in the English language, his works have withstood the test of time. The study of Shakespeare's plays inevitably leads to the question, "What was Shakespeare trying to achieve?" Although the answer to this question is pure speculation, it is safe to assume that he was trying to fully realize the "tragic hero" that he had begun developing near the beginning of his career in the character of the Machiavellian Richard III. Later, in *Titus Andronicus*, Shakespeare made his tragic hero not only scheming but brutal as well. He continued to perfect the tragic hero in other plays, creating the characters of Hamlet, Othello, King Lear, and Marcus Brutus in *Julius Caesar*. Some critics see the character of Macbeth as the perfect

Shakespearean tragic hero: brooding and torn by conflicting emotions but ultimately fallible as a result of the human quality of ambition. Macbeth is a hero who consciously pursues a course of action despite the fact that it will mean his downfall.

Macbeth is also Shakespeare's most concentrated study of evil. From the beginning, the audience knows that Macbeth is doomed, and it holds its collective breath as Macbeth moves from one horrible murder to the next. The audience is relieved at the end of the play when Macduff finally kills Macbeth and presents his head to Malcolm.

This study of evil also helped Shakespeare expand the genre of tragedy to its ultimate limit of good versus evil. In *Macbeth* the audience is treated to a morality play in which evil, in the forms of Macbeth, Lady Macbeth, and the Weird Sisters, temporarily triumphs over good, symbolized by the character of King Duncan. However, the righteous avengers, Malcolm and Macduff, are ultimately victorious. The moral of the play, which is still used to this day in movies and television shows, is that no evil deed will go unpunished.

Although the history of Shakespeare's *Macbeth* is filled with superstition, mishaps, and centuries of failed performances, it remains one of the bard's most-discussed, and loved, plays. Some critics have hailed *Macbeth* as the perfect tragedy, but others have dismissed it as an impure work that was changed by unknown

Orson Welles appears as Macbeth in the 1948 movie version of the play.

writers. Despite the cursed reputation of the play, it is still occasionally performed on the stage, and it has been made into several movies. The continuing appeal of *Macbeth* can be traced to its unflinching depiction of evil and the psychological insight that Shakespeare displays in the guilt-wracked characters of Macbeth and his wife.

CHAPTER THREE

The Plot of *Macbeth:* A Study of Evil

M *acbeth* is the last, and the darkest, of Shakespeare's four great tragedies (*Hamlet, Othello,* and *King Lear*). As scholar Frank Kermode observes, "In no other play does Shakespeare show a nation so cruelly occupied by the powers of darkness; and *Macbeth* is . . . his most intensive study of evil at work in the individual and in the world at large."²⁶ The character of Macbeth grows in evil throughout the play after being infected with the venomous promises of the Weird Sisters. Each scene brings a new act of villainy from Macbeth, who is encouraged by Lady Macbeth. Macbeth and his wife weave a web of violence that eventually ensnares them and causes their own bloody downfalls.

The brooding evil of *Macbeth* is at least due in part to the setting of the play. The Scottish moor is just as dark and forbidding as the subject matter of the play. Almost all of the action takes place at night or in the dark of early morning while the play is constantly lashed by wind, thunder, and rain. In *Macbeth* Shakespeare uses the setting of the play to foreshadow the darkness and confusion that is about to fall on Scotland and Macbeth.

Act 1, Scenes 1 and 2: The Witches and the Battle

Macbeth, like many of Shakespeare's plays, begins *media res* (Latin for "in the middle of things"). The three Weird Sisters enter amid a clap of thunder and a flash of lightning and against the backdrop of a battle that Macbeth is currently fighting. One sister asks, "When shall we three meet again? / In thunder, lightning, or in rain?" Another sister answers, "When the hurly-burly's done, / When the battle's lost and won." These opening lines establish the play's dark setting, supernatural elements, and use of equivocation. The Weird Sisters agree to meet on the heath at sunset and approach Macbeth. The sisters then call their familiars and exit with the equivocal phrase, "Fair is foul, and foul is fair." [27]

Scene 2 begins with King Duncan, accompanied by his sons, Malcolm and Donalbain, entering a military camp a short distance from the battle. The men find a bleeding sergeant who reports that the battle started off badly but was rescued by Macbeth, who reached the rebel Macdonwald and killed him. The sergeant concludes his report by describing how the Norwegian king (Macdonwald's ally), thinking he had the advantage, attacked Macbeth and Banquo with fresh troops, and that currently Macbeth and Banquo were trying to fight him off. The sergeant is overcome by his wounds and is helped off the stage.

As the sergeant exits, Rosse and Angus, fresh from the front, enter and salute King Duncan. Rosse reports that even though the king's forces were outnumbered by the Norwegians and the treacherous thane of Cawdor, Macbeth's military skill won the day. Rosse further reports that the Norwegian king is suing for peace and has already paid Macbeth ten thousand dollars. King Duncan is overjoyed to hear this news and decides to execute the thane of Cawdor and award his title to Macbeth. King Duncan orders Rosse to seek out Macbeth and greet him with the title.

Act 1, Scene 3: Macbeth and Banquo Meet the Weird Sisters

The action of the play then shifts to the Scottish heath, where the Weird Sisters have regrouped and await Macbeth's arrival.

Macbeth and Banquo encounter the Weird Sisters on a deserted heath.

Macbeth and Banquo enter, and Macbeth states (closely parallel-
ing act 1, scene 1, line 11) "So foul and fair a day I have not
seen." [28] Banquo is the first to see the Weird Sisters and is shocked
because he cannot tell if they are men or women. The Sisters
greet Macbeth as the "Thane of Glamis," the "Thane of
Cawdor," and "King hereafter." [29] Macbeth is shocked by this
greeting, and Banquo chides him by asking, "Why do you start,
and seem to fear / Things that do sound so fair?" [30] Banquo then
asks the Weird Sisters what the future holds for him, and they

reply that he shall be "lesser than Macbeth, and greater" and "not so happy, yet much happier." They conclude their prophecy by telling Banquo that "thou shalt get kings, though thou be none."[31] Macbeth tries to question the Weird Sisters further, but they vanish.

Rosse and Angus enter at this point. Rosse tells Macbeth that King Duncan has awarded Macbeth the title thane of Cawdor. Macbeth and Banquo are shocked by this news, and Macbeth wonders about the truthfulness of the sisters' other predictions. Banquo cautions him that "oftentimes, to win us to our harm, / The instruments of darkness tell us truths, / Win us with honest trifles, to betray us / In deepest consequence."[32] Macbeth begins to ponder the prospect of becoming king by murdering Duncan, but he eventually finds the idea unappealing. Before Macbeth and Banquo exit with Rosse and Angus, Macbeth pulls Banquo aside and asks to speak with him later.

Act 1, Scene 4: King Duncan Names Malcolm as His Heir

King Duncan and his sons, Malcolm and Donalbain, are discussing the execution of the traitorous thane of Cawdor when Macbeth, Banquo, Rosse, and Angus enter. King Duncan praises Macbeth and states that he is forever in Macbeth's debt; he then praises Banquo in the same way. King Duncan then declares to his assembled kinsmen and subjects that his son Malcolm will be the heir to the throne of Scotland. The news is a blow to Macbeth, but he covers his shock by inviting the king and his entourage to his castle at Glamis to celebrate. Once he is away from the crowd, Macbeth describes his frustration at this new development in a soliloquy.

Act 1, Scene 5: Lady Macbeth Learns of the Weird Sisters' Predictions

Lady Macbeth enters a room at Glamis castle reading aloud from a letter that Macbeth has sent her describing the prophecies of the Weird Sisters. Although Lady Macbeth is glad to hear the news, she fears that Macbeth may be "too full o' th' milk of human kindness" to do what it takes to win the crown, and she feels that she must encourage him. Lady Macbeth cannot believe the opportunity that has fallen into her lap. She quickly embraces the idea of murdering King Duncan and cries out, "Come, you spirits / That tend on mortal thoughts, unsex me here, / And fill me from the crown to the toe topful / Of direst cruelty!"[33] She then asks that her mother's milk be replaced by gall, and she invokes the night to aid her.

As she is finishing the thought, Macbeth enters the room. Lady Macbeth greets her husband enthusiastically and he repeats the news that King Duncan will be arriving shortly. Lady Macbeth counsels her husband to "bear welcome in your eye, / Your hand, your tongue; look like the innocent flower, / But be the serpent under't."[34] Macbeth only replies that they will discuss the subject later.

Act 1, Scene 6: King Duncan Is Welcomed to Macbeth's Castle

As King Duncan, Malcolm, Donalbain, Banquo, and other lords and attendants enter Macbeth's castle at Glamis, Duncan comments to Banquo about how sweet the air is. Banquo responds that the air is indeed sweeter around Macbeth's castle. Lady Macbeth greets her royal guest with a polite and flattering welcome. She then conducts King Duncan into the castle.

Act 1, Scene 7: Lady Macbeth Convinces Macbeth to Murder Duncan

This scene begins with Macbeth's soliloquy in which he debates the idea of murdering King Duncan. The idea at first appeals to Macbeth, but only if the murderous act "might be the be-all and the end-all."[35] However, Macbeth realizes that he would be inviting his own downfall by killing Duncan. Macbeth recounts King Duncan's good qualities and decides that murdering him would be a crime against nature. Just as Macbeth resolves not to kill the king, Lady Macbeth enters.

Macbeth tells his wife, "We will proceed no further in this business"[36] because he has no intention of dishonoring himself. Lady

Macbeth tells him that he lacks the courage to act upon his desires. She retorts that Macbeth is not a man because he raised her expectations only to dash them. Macbeth asks her what they would do if they fail. She replies, "We fail? / But screw your courage to the sticking place, / And we'll not fail"[37] and she then describes the plan for killing Duncan: They will get the king's chamberlains drunk, and while Duncan sleeps, they will kill him and blame it on the drunken servants. Macbeth is shocked at the cold-bloodedness of Lady Macbeth and tells her, "Bring forth men-children only! / For thy undaunted mettle should compose / Nothing but males."[38] However, he agrees to murder the king.

Lady Macbeth convinces her husband to murder King Duncan.

Act 2, Scene 1: Macbeth Sees a Dagger That Leads Him Toward Duncan's Room

It is after midnight in Macbeth's castle, and Fleance is leading his father, Banquo, to his room for the night. Banquo and his son are surprised by Macbeth and a servant in the dark. Banquo tells Macbeth that he has dreamed of the Weird Sisters, but Macbeth lies and tells Banquo that he has not thought about them. Macbeth subtly suggests that if Banquo were to support him for the kingship he would be rewarded. Banquo replies that he will support Macbeth as long as it does not threaten his honor. As Banquo and Fleance exit, Macbeth dismisses his servant to find out if Lady Macbeth has his "drink" ready.

Once Macbeth is alone, a dagger appears to him, but he cannot decide whether it is real or if it is "a dagger of the mind, a false creation, / Proceeding from the heat-oppressed brain."[39] The dagger then leads Macbeth in the direction of King Duncan's room. Macbeth hears Lady Macbeth ringing a bell and exits the stage toward the sleeping king.

Act 2, Scene 2: The Murder of Duncan

Lady Macbeth waits outside King Duncan's room while Macbeth murders the king. While waiting, she is startled by the sound of an owl. Lady Macbeth is further shaken by the sound of Macbeth at "work" in the chamber and fears that they will be discovered.

Macbeth enters and states, "I have done the deed." He looks at his hands, bloody from the murder, and comments, "This is a sorry sight." Lady Macbeth tells him to be quiet, but he tells her how the chamberlains awakened from their sleep, said a prayer, and then went back to sleep. He tells his wife that as he murdered King Duncan he heard a voice cry: "Sleep no more! / Macbeth does murder sleep."[40] Lady Macbeth tells her husband to get a hold of himself and wash the blood from his hands. She asks

Macbeth, with a dagger in his hand, prepares to murder King Duncan.

After smearing the chamberlains with blood, Lady Macbeth shows Macbeth her bloodstained hands.

Macbeth why he brought the daggers from the room and tells him to take them back in there and smear the chamberlains with blood. Macbeth refuses and Lady Macbeth insults him, telling him that she will do it herself. She enters King Duncan's chamber.

Macbeth, left alone, hears a knocking and then begins to ponder his bloodstained hands. Lady Macbeth reenters and shows Macbeth her own bloodstained hands. She hears the knocking that Macbeth had heard earlier and hurries him from the room. The knocking grows louder and more persistent as Macbeth and his wife exit. Macbeth idly wishes that the knocking would awaken the murdered king.

Act 2, Scene 3: The Discovery of Duncan's Murder

The knocking at the gate is answered by the porter, or doorman, and thus begins one of Shakespeare's famous comic scenes. The porter of Macbeth's castle is irritated at being awakened at such an ungodly hour (just before dawn) after a night of drinking. The porter imagines himself as the keeper of the gates of hell, opening the gates for various sinners. The porter then complains that Macbeth's castle is too cold and too noisy to be hell. As the porter opens the door, he begs the audience to "remember the porter."[41]

Macduff and Lennox enter Macbeth's castle. Macduff is clearly irritated about being kept waiting outside and rebukes the porter for his tardiness. The porter pleads drunkenness and lures Macduff into a joke. The two men trade jests one more time, and Macduff asks the porter if Macbeth is awake.

At that moment Macbeth enters dressed in his nightgown, and Macduff asks him if King Duncan is awake. Macbeth replies that the king still sleeps, and Macduff exits to wake him. Lennox comments to Macbeth about how stormy the night has been and how he heard strange voices and screams in the wind. Macbeth agrees that it was indeed a rough night.

Macduff reenters suddenly and shouts, "O horror, horror, horror! Tongue nor heart / Cannot conceive or name thee!" Macduff, despite the prodding of Macbeth and Lennox, cannot tell them that the king has been murdered. Instead, he tells them "Approach the chamber, and destroy your sight / With a new Gorgon. Do not bid me speak; / See, and then speak yourselves."[42] Macbeth and Lennox exit to see what has happened while Macduff calls for the bell to be rung and awakes the castle with his shouting.

Lady Macbeth enters and asks what the uproar is about, but Macduff tells her that it is not for a woman's ears to hear. When Banquo enters, Macduff blurts out, "Our royal master's murther'd!"[43] Macbeth, Lennox, and Rosse reenter, and Macbeth expresses his sorrow about Duncan's murder. Malcolm and Donalbain, King Duncan's sons, enter and are informed that their father is dead and that the killers seem to be his chamberlains. At this point Macbeth confesses that the sight of the murdered King caused him to kill the obviously guilty chamberlains in a fit of passion. Lady Macbeth then faints.

As Lady Macbeth is carried out, Banquo tells the gathered crowd that they should meet to "question this most bloody piece of work" and find the root of the "treasonous malice."[44] The crowd vows to support Banquo, and they all leave to meet in the hall to figure out a course of action. Malcolm and Donalbain remain behind to discuss their father's death. They decide that it would be safer if they went their separate ways rather than lingering where "there's daggers in men's smiles."[45] Malcolm, Duncan's designated heir, decides to flee to England, and Donalbain decides to escape to Ireland.

Act 2, Scene 4: Rosse and an Old Man Discuss Current Events

A short time later, Rosse talks with an old man outside of Macbeth's castle. The old man states that in his seventy years he has seen many terrible and strange things, "but this sore night / Hath trifled former knowings."[46] Rosse comments on the unnatural darkness of the day, and the old man adds that he has noticed the birds acting strangely. Rosse then describes how the king's horses have turned wild and have been attacking each other.

Macduff enters and Rosse asks him if they have discovered the murderer. Macduff responds by telling him that it is "those that Macbeth hath slain"[47] and that Malcolm and Donalbain have fled, which makes them look suspicious. Rosse speculates that the crown of Scotland will fall to Macbeth, and Macduff confirms that Macbeth has already been named and is on his way to the coronation.

Act 3, Scene 1: Macbeth Orders Banquo's Murder

Act 3 begins in the king's palace in Forres, Scotland. Banquo enters alone and voices his concerns about Macbeth in a short speech: "Thou hast it now: King, Cawdor, Glamis, all, / As the weird women promis'd, and I fear / Thou play'dst most foully for't."[48] Macbeth and his wife enter, dressed in royal robes and attended by Lennox, Rosse, and other lords and ladies.

Macbeth greets Banquo and asks if he will attend a supper that Macbeth is hosting that night. Banquo claims that he has business that must be taken care of and asks Macbeth to forgive his rudeness. When Macbeth inquires about Banquo's destination, Banquo offers an evasive answer. Macbeth informs Banquo that Malcolm and Donalbain have safely escaped and are claiming that Macbeth murdered their father. Macbeth bids Banquo good-bye and then dismisses the gathered court until the supper.

Macbeth asks a servant to bring some waiting men to him. After the servant leaves, Macbeth voices his suspicions about Banquo and accuses Banquo of only seeking the crown for himself. Macbeth then curses the Weird Sisters because "upon my head they plac'd a fruitless crown, / And put a barren scepter in my grip, / Thence to be wrench'd with an unlineal hand, / No son of mine succeeding."[49] Macbeth states that he did not condemn his soul so that Banquo's descendants could inherit the throne.

The servant interrupts Macbeth's musings and announces the entrance of the two men he had been sent to fetch. Macbeth sends the servant away and greets the two men abruptly. Macbeth reveals to the men how Banquo was responsible for their past misfortunes. He finally asks them, "Do you find / Your patience so predominant in your nature / That you can let this go?"[50] One of the men responds, "We are men, my liege,"[51] which leads Macbeth to question their manhood in the same way his wife questioned his earlier in act 1, scene 7. Macbeth asks them if they are men enough to go through with the murder of Banquo. Both respond that they are firmly committed to his death. Macbeth explains that he cannot kill Banquo himself because he would lose the loyalty of Banquo's friends. Macbeth commends the soon-to-be murderers and tells them where and when they will kill Banquo. Macbeth then adds that they should kill Fleance, Banquo's son, as well. The murderers affirm that they will do a good job, and Macbeth dismisses them.

Act 3, Scene 2: Macbeth and Lady Macbeth Discuss the Problem of Banquo

In another room of the royal palace at Forres, Lady Macbeth asks a servant to summon Macbeth. When Macbeth enters, Lady Macbeth asks him why he keeps to himself and dwells on the murder of Duncan. She tells Macbeth, "Things without all remedy / Should be without regard: what's done, is done."[52]

Macbeth warns his wife, "We have scorch'd the snake, not kill'd it,"[53] and tells her that the murder may come back to haunt them. Macbeth comments that he would rather be dead than to live in fear and sleep with nightmares. Lady Macbeth attempts to cajole him, but he will not be jovial.

At this point Lady Macbeth implores Macbeth to halt this line of thinking. He reminds his wife that Banquo and Fleance still live, but he vows that before the night is over "a deed of dreadful note" will be done. Lady Macbeth asks what Macbeth has in mind, but he tells her she would be better off not knowing. Macbeth then invokes the night to cover up the "tender eye of day" so that "night's black agents"[54] can perform their evil actions.

Act 3, Scene 3: The Murder of Banquo

In a wooded park outside of the royal palace, the two murderers are joined by a third murderer sent by Macbeth. When Banquo and Fleance approach, the three murderers surprise them, and Banquo urges his son to "fly, good Fleance, fly, fly, fly! / Thou mayest revenge."[55] During the short fight with the murderers, the light goes out and Fleance manages to escape in the confusion and darkness. Banquo, however, is killed. The three men realize that they have only accomplished half of their mission, but they resolve to inform Macbeth anyway.

Act 3, Scene 4: Banquo's Ghost Appears at the Banquet

In the dining hall of the royal palace, Macbeth welcomes his subjects to the banquet. Macbeth then sees one of the murderers appear at a side door, so he urges everyone to sit down while he discreetly approaches the man. "There's blood upon thy face," [56] Macbeth comments. The murderer replies, "'Tis Banquo's then." [57] Macbeth then asks if Fleance has been killed as well, and the murderer reports that Fleance has escaped. Macbeth is disappointed, but he is reassured that at least Banquo is dead. Macbeth then dismisses the murderer and returns to the banquet, where he is scolded by his wife for not being merry.

Unnoticed by Macbeth, and unseen by the gathered nobility, Banquo's ghost enters the room and sits in Macbeth's place at the table. Lennox invites Macbeth to sit at the table, but Macbeth, who is the only character who can see the ghost, thinks the table is full. When Macbeth asks again where he should sit, Lennox gestures to the chair occupied by Banquo's ghost. Macbeth now recognizes the ghost as Banquo. At first thinking that one of the nobles is behind the ghost of Banquo, he shouts at them, "Which of you have done this?" The nobles, who cannot see the ghost, do not know what Macbeth is talking about. Realizing that it really is the ghost of Banquo, Macbeth tells it, "Thou canst not say I did it; never shake thy gory locks at me." [58] Rosse tries to get the gathered nobles to leave, but Lady Macbeth stops them and tells them that it is a momentary affliction, something Macbeth has suffered from since youth.

She takes Macbeth aside and tells him that the ghost of Banquo is a "painting of [his] fear" [59] like the ghastly dagger that led him to the murder of Duncan. Macbeth asks if anybody else can see the ghost, and then he commands the ghost to speak. The ghost exits.

Lady Macbeth mocks him, and Macbeth protests that the ghost was indeed present. Lady Macbeth realizes that their conversation is being overheard and that their guests are staring at them. She gently draws Macbeth's attention to this, and he tells them that he is suffering from a "strange infirmity." [60]

Macbeth proposes a toast, and while his glass is filled with wine, the ghost of Banquo enters the room again. Macbeth loses his composure again and addresses the ghost in front of everybody: "Avaunt, and quit my sight! let the earth hide thee! / Thy bones are marrowless, thy blood is cold; / Thou hast no speculation in those eyes / Which thou dost glare with!"[61] Lady Macbeth once again tries to explain away the outburst, and Macbeth orders the ghost to leave, which it does.

Lady Macbeth chastises Macbeth for breaking the mood of the banquet, but he wonders how the others can see the ghost and not turn pale. When one of the nobles, Rosse, attempts to question Macbeth about what he saw, Lady Macbeth tells him to stop because the questions aggravate Macbeth's condition, and she orders the nobles to leave. Once the nobles have exited, Macbeth asks his wife why Macduff did not attend the banquet. Lady Macbeth asks if he sent for Macduff, and Macbeth replies that he has heard that Macduff is suspicious of him. Macbeth then reveals that he plans to visit the Weird Sisters the next day to find out more about the predictions. The two then exit the dining hall.

Act 3, Scene 5: The Weird Sisters Meet with Hecat

(This scene was probably not written by Shakespeare and was likely added to the play later by Thomas Middleton.) The Weird Sisters meet with Hecat, the devil they serve, on the Scottish heath. One of the sisters asks why Hecat looks so angry, and she responds that she is angry because the sisters have been prophesying to Macbeth without her permission. Hecat then commands the Weird Sisters to meet her in the morning because Macbeth is going to seek them out to know his destiny, and Hecat is determined to draw him deeper into the web of evil. At this point, there is singing and dancing by the Weird Sisters, Hecat, and other cast members. At the end of the song, all of the characters exit.

Act 3, Scene 6: Lennox and Another Scottish Lord Discuss Current Events

Somewhere in Scotland, Lennox meets another Scottish lord and the two men discuss the recent events. Lennox recounts how he believes Malcolm and Donalbain fled after they murdered their father, Duncan, and how Fleance has fled after killing his father, Banquo. Lennox goes on to explain how Macbeth killed the two men who supposedly carried out the murder of Duncan. He adds that if Macbeth had Duncan's sons and Fleance under lock and key he would surely punish them for murdering their fathers. Lennox then asks about Macduff's whereabouts.

The Scottish lord reports that Macduff has joined Malcolm in England under the protection of the English king, Edward. The Scottish lord explains that Macduff went to England to seek aid in overthrowing Macbeth, and that Macbeth has heard this news and is preparing for war. Lennox suggests that Macduff is wise to stay away from Macbeth and suggests that somebody should send a message to England warning Macduff about Macbeth.

Act 4, Scene 1: Macbeth Meets with the Weird Sisters for the Second Time

The Weird Sisters gather in a cave somewhere in Scotland and begin to weave their charm over a boiling cauldron. They chant as they stir the ingredients into the unholy mixture. Eventually Hecat appears to commend their preparations and then vanishes again. One of the Weird Sisters senses Macbeth's presence and announces his arrival: "By the pricking of my thumbs, / Something wicked this way comes."[62]

Macbeth enters the Weird Sisters' cave and demands that they answer his questions. The sisters tell Macbeth that they will answer any questions he may ask, or he can get the answers directly from their masters. Macbeth tells the sisters to call their masters, and they pour sow's blood into the boiling cauldron: the first apparition, an armed head, appears.

"Macbeth! Macbeth! Macbeth!" calls the first apparition, "beware Macduff, / Beware the Thane of Fife. Dismiss me. Enough."[63] Macbeth thanks the first apparition for confirming his own suspicions. In a clap of thunder, the second apparition, a bloody child, appears. The second apparition tells Macbeth to

The Weird Sisters meet Macbeth for a second time and conjure up three apparitions that tell him of his future.

"be bloody, bold, and resolute: laugh to scorn / The pow'r of man; for none of woman born / Shall harm Macbeth."[64] Macbeth gloats over the news. In another clap of thunder, the third apparition appears, a crowned child with a tree in his hand, and tells Macbeth to "be lion-mettled, proud, and take no care / Who chafes, who frets, or where conspirers are; / Macbeth shall never vanquish'd be until / Great Birnan wood to high Dunsinane hill / Shall come against him."[65] Macbeth rejoices at this announcement because he believes that it is impossible for the woods to move onto the hill.

However, this is not enough for Macbeth. He wants to know more, and so he asks if Banquo's descendants will ever rule Scotland. The Weird Sisters try to dissuade him from this question, but Macbeth demands to be satisfied. The Weird Sisters comply, and a vision of eight kings appears. The eighth king is holding a mirror that shows even more kings, some of them holding the symbols of Scotland, England, and Ireland. One of the apparitions appears to be Banquo. Macbeth is dismayed by this sight and asks if the line will go on forever. After the apparitions vanish, the Weird Sisters perform a dance and disappear.

Macbeth then summons Lennox inside and asks him if he saw the sisters leave. Lennox reports that he saw no one leave, and he discloses that Macduff had fled to England. Macbeth is shocked that Macduff has already escaped, but he determines that he will kill Macduff's wife and children. Macbeth then exits the cave to fulfill his plan.

Act 4, Scene 2: The Massacre of Macduff's Family

At Macduff's castle, Lady Macduff questions Rosse about why her husband had to flee Scotland and "leave his wife, his babes, / His mansion and his titles, in a place / From whence himself does fly?"[66] Rosse asks Lady Macduff to control herself and adds that her husband "is noble, wise, judicious, and best knows / The fits o' th' season."[67] Rosse then excuses himself, but he promises to return soon.

Shortly after, a messenger enters and tells Lady Macduff that "some danger does approach you nearly. / If you will take a homely man's advice, / Be not found here."[68] Before Lady Macduff can question the messenger further, he again advises her to take her children and escape, and then he flees himself. As Lady Macduff tries to decide what to do, some men burst into the room and demand her husband's whereabouts. Lady Macduff refuses to cooperate, and the men stab her son when he tries to intervene in her defense. Lady Macduff flees the room screaming while pursued by the murderers.

Act 4, Scene 3: Malcolm and Macduff Meet in England

Malcolm and Macduff meet at King Edward's palace in England. Malcolm suggests that they go apart and weep, but Macduff insists that they discuss the recent events in Scotland. Malcolm ambiguously responds that he will do what he can to help Scotland, and he lets Macduff know that he is suspicious of his motives for visiting. Macduff protests that he is not treacherous but Malcolm reminds him that Macbeth is. Macduff laments that all hope is lost. Meanwhile, Malcolm (who is trying to figure out if Macduff is a friend or foe) asks him why he left his wife and children in Scotland. Malcolm tells Macduff that he shares his concern about the future of Scotland and reveals that England has already offered to help him overthrow Macbeth, but he feels that Scotland is better off under Macbeth than himself.

Malcolm admits that his own sins are so great as to make "black Macbeth / . . . seem as pure as snow."[69] Malcolm proceeds to explain his own lust and greed. Malcolm, still not sure if Macduff is a friend or foe, eventually claims that he possesses none of the kingly graces and has no desire to develop them.

Macduff has finally had enough. He tells Malcolm that he is not fit to govern, let alone to live. Macduff grieves for Scotland and wonders when it will see "wholesome days again."[70] Malcolm, now convinced of Macduff's integrity, reveals that he was testing Macduff and that everything he said about himself was false. Malcolm states that he is ready to serve Macduff and Scotland, and that old Siward (the earl of Northumberland and the general of the English army) has ten thousand men ready to march on Macbeth.

Macduff is a little shocked at the sudden turn of events, and while he is pondering the situation Rosse enters. Rosse tells the men that Scotland has become a living hell. Malcolm and Macduff are dismayed to hear this news, and Macduff asks about his family. Rosse confesses that he has brought some heavy news: Macbeth is preparing for war in Scotland and impressing citizens into his army. But Rosse says he has even heavier news: "Your castle is supris'd; your wife, and babes, / Savagely slaughtered."[71] Macduff is overcome by grief and blames himself for the murder of his family. He vows to kill Macbeth. Malcolm informs Macduff and Rosse that everything is ready for their march on Scotland and Macbeth.

Act 5, Scene 1: Lady Macbeth's Sleepwalking

The first scene of act 5 opens in Macbeth's castle on Dunsinane Hill in Scotland, where a waiting gentlewoman is consulting a Scots doctor about Lady Macbeth's sleepwalking. The gentlewoman reveals that every night Lady Macbeth rises from her bed, dresses, unlocks her closet, retrieves paper, writes on it, reads it, seals it, and returns to bed without waking. The doctor suggests that this signals a "great perturbation in [her] nature."[72]

At that moment Lady Macbeth enters carrying a lighted candle. The doctor asks about the candle, and the gentlewoman explains that Lady Macbeth has commanded that she have light continually. The doctor and the gentlewoman watch as Lady Macbeth rubs her hands as if washing them. Addressing the imagined bloodstains on her hands, Lady Macbeth curses them: "Out, damn'd spot! out I say!" A little bit later, the sleepwalking Lady Macbeth shocks the doctor when she wonders, "Yet who would have thought the old man to have had so much blood in him?"[73] While Lady Macbeth continues to make incriminating statements in her sleep, the doctor tells the gentlewoman that "this disease is beyond my practice."[74] They continue to watch Lady Macbeth reenact Duncan's murder in a haphazard fashion until she exits. The doctor commands the gentlewoman to watch after Lady Macbeth. The two characters then bid each other goodnight.

Act 5, Scene 2: Rebel Scottish Lords Abandon Macbeth

In a field near Macbeth's stronghold, a group of Scottish noblemen and their armies meet. One of the Scottish nobles, Menteth, reports that the English army is nearby and led by Malcolm, Siward, and Macduff. Angus, another Scottish noble, reveals that they are supposed to meet the English forces near Birnan Wood. Menteth asks what Macbeth is up to, and Cathness, another noble, replies that he is adding to the defenses of Dunsinane Hill.

This 1928 production of Macbeth *shows a sleepwalking Lady Macbeth in contemporary dress.*

The men resolve to march on and "give obedience where 'tis truly ow'd"[75] and meet Malcolm, Macduff, and the English forces near Birnan Wood.

Act 5, Scene 3: Macbeth Learns of the Approaching English Army and His Wife's Illness

In his castle atop Dunsinane Hill, Macbeth is in a foul mood. He reminds himself that Malcolm is born of a woman and that the

Weird Sisters promised him that no man born of a woman shall harm him. A servant appears and reports that the English army numbers ten thousand soldiers. Macbeth reconciles himself to battle and calls for his squire Seyton. Seyton confirms the reports from the field, and Macbeth vows, "I'll fight, till from my bones my flesh be hack'd."[76] Macbeth orders Seyton to help him into his armor.

While Seyton is strapping Macbeth into his armor, Macbeth asks the doctor how his wife is doing. The doctor reports that Lady Macbeth is not physically ill, but instead is "troubled with thick-coming fantasies, / That keep her from her rest." Macbeth commands the doctor to cure his wife, but the doctor protests that "the patient / Must minister to himself."[77] Macbeth then condemns medicine as useless and exits while Seyton is still trying to strap him into his armor.

Act 5, Scene 4: Malcolm Orders His Soldiers to Cut Branches from the Trees of Birnan Wood

In a field near Birnan Wood, the disgruntled subjects of Macbeth (Menteth, Cathness, Angus, and Lennox) meet the English forces led by Malcolm, Siward, Macduff, and Rosse. Malcolm orders that every soldier chop down a tree and carry it before him as the army approaches Macbeth's stronghold to conceal their numbers. Siward observes that Macbeth seems content to allow the English army to lay siege to his castle, and Malcolm points out that nobody is fighting with Macbeth because they want to, but rather because they have been forced into service. The men decide that now is the time for action, and they begin marching toward Macbeth's castle on Dunsinane Hill.

Act 5, Scene 5: Macbeth Learns of his Wife's Suicide and the Approach of Birnan Wood

Macbeth is on the ramparts of his castle and is confident that he can hold off the English army. However, his musings are interrupted by the cries of women. Macbeth sends Seyton to find the cause of the cries. Seyton returns and reports that the queen is dead. Macbeth is emotionless at the news of his wife's death and wishes only that she had died later. He meditates on the meaning of life and decides that it is a "walking shadow, a poor player, / That struts and frets his hour upon the stage, / And then is heard no more. It is a tale / Told by an idiot, full of sound and fury, / Signifying nothing."[78]

A messenger disrupts Macbeth's thoughts with the news that Birnan Wood is moving toward Macbeth's castle. Macbeth calls the messenger a "liar and a slave"[79] and threatens to hang him from a tree. The messenger protests that he is telling the truth, and Macbeth begins to question the honesty of the Weird Sisters. Macbeth orders his forces out of the castle and into the field for battle.

Act 5, Scenes 6 and 7: The Battle for Scotland Begins

In a field before Macbeth's castle, Malcolm orders his soldiers to drop the trees and reveal themselves. He then asks Siward and his son to lead the first charge while he and Macduff encircle the flank.

Meanwhile, across the field Macbeth realizes that he is trapped. In the midst of the battle, Siward's son, known in the play as "young Siward," crosses Macbeth's path and challenges Macbeth to fight. Macbeth slays young Siward in the ensuing battle and laughs over his corpse: "But swords I smile at, weapons laugh to scorn, / Brandish'd by man that's of a woman born."[80] Macbeth then stalks off to look for another enemy.

Macduff enters shortly after Macbeth exits. He calls out for Macbeth: "Tyrant, show thy face!"[81] Macduff states that he is tired of fighting Macbeth's hirelings and wants to fight Macbeth himself. Macduff invokes fortune to aid him and exits looking for Macbeth.

Act 5, Scene 8: Macbeth and Macduff's Duel

Macbeth once again crosses the field of battle, but this time he crosses paths with Macduff. Macduff challenges him, but Macbeth tries to warn him away: "Of all men else I have avoided thee. / But get thee back, my soul is too much charg'd / With blood of thine already." Macduff refuses to retreat and the two men fight. They stop fighting for a moment and Macbeth tells Macduff, "I bear a charmed life, which must not yield / To one of woman born." [82] Macduff laughs at Macbeth: "Despair thy charm, / . . . Macduff was from his mother's womb / Untimely ripp'd." [83]

Macbeth curses Macduff because his revelation has caused Macbeth to realize his folly in believing the Weird Sisters. Macbeth refuses to fight Macduff, and Macduff asks him to surrender. Macbeth states that he will not yield; he will try until the last. Macbeth and Macduff exit fighting, there are alarms, and the two men reenter fighting. Macbeth is slain, and Macduff exits dragging Macbeth's body.

Act 5, Scene 9: The Triumph of Malcolm and Macduff

Malcolm, Siward, Rosse, and the other Scottish lords enter a room in Macbeth's castle. Macduff enters the room with Macbeth's head and greets Malcolm: "Hail, King! For so thou art. Behold where stands / Th' usurper's head." [84] Macduff then presents the kingdom to Malcolm and hails him again as the king of Scotland. Malcolm addresses the crowd, thanking his friends for helping him, and promotes them to earls. Malcolm then recalls all Scottish exiles and promises to weed out all the "cruel ministers / Of this dead butcher and his fiend-like queen." [85] Malcolm then invites the crowd to his crowning at Scone.

CHAPTER FOUR

The
Characters of
Macbeth

W illiam Shakespeare's tragedies are known for their tragic heroes, but the bard often used the actions of minor characters to move the plays to their tragic conclusions. *Macbeth* typifies Shakespeare's tragedies because, although the imposing figure of Macbeth dominates the play, the actions of the other characters, some of whom change allegiance, move the drama to its ultimate conclusion. Rosse and Lennox are two minor characters in *Macbeth* who act as "go-betweens," relaying information between the main characters and driving the play to its climax. Macduff starts the play as a minor character, but he evolves into the avenger who will return the throne of Scotland to its rightful owner, Malcolm.

The tragedy of Macbeth is also made more poignant because of the depth of the relationships between the characters. Macbeth murders his cousin Duncan and plans the murder of his friend Banquo and his son, Fleance. The slaying of Lady Macduff and her children shocks the audience and spurs Macduff to join forces with Malcolm to overthrow Macbeth. In fact, *Macbeth* is a play in which the characters are just as important as the plot.

Banquo

Banquo is a Scottish nobleman, a general in the Scottish army, a friend to Macbeth, and Macbeth's foil (dramatic opposite). The character of Banquo is introduced in act 1, scene 2 as he battles with Macbeth against the Norwegians and rebel Scots. Banquo is also with Macbeth when he first meets the Weird Sisters. In addition to predicting Macbeth's future, the Weird Sisters prophesy to Banquo that "thou shalt get kings, though thou be none"[86]— that is, he will be the father of kings although he will not be one himself. Unlike Macbeth, Banquo is very suspicious of the Weird Sisters and warns Macbeth about them early in the play. Later, when Macbeth hints that Banquo would be rewarded for supporting him in his bid for the throne in the event of Duncan's death, Banquo responds that he will support Macbeth as long as he loses no honor.

Macbeth fears, and eventually kills, Banquo because of this virtue: "Our fears in Banquo / Stick deep, and in his royalty of nature / Reigns that which would be fear'd."[87] Unlike Macbeth's ambition, Banquo's is checked by his loyalty and honor. Even after his death, Banquo continues to threaten Macbeth in the form of a ghost. In fact, he causes Macbeth to lose his composure at his dinner party. Shakespearean scholar Victor L. Cahn has stated that "Banquo is not immune to ambition, but such steadfastness in the face of temptation contrasts with Macbeth's yielding."[88] In other words, Banquo is tempted by the Weird Sisters but unlike Macbeth, he does not give in to his ambition.

Donalbain

Donalbain is the youngest son of Duncan, the king of Scotland. Donalbain is silent for most of the first two acts of *Macbeth*, but he finally finds his tongue after his father is murdered. Fearing for his life and that of his brother, Malcolm, after their father's murder, Donalbain asks Malcolm why they should remain in Scotland, "where our fate, / Hid in an auger-hole, may rush and seize us?" The brothers agree that their "separated fortune / Shall keep us both safer," [89] and Donalbain volunteers to go to Ireland while his brother goes to England. Although Donalbain does not appear in the play again, he is briefly mentioned in act 5, scene 2 when one of the rebelling Scottish lords, Cathness, asks if Donalbain is with Malcolm. Apparently, Donalbain decides to stay in Ireland while his brother defeats Macbeth. Donalbain's character serves the purpose of setting up the opportunity for Malcolm to return from England with an army to overthrow Macbeth.

Duncan, King of Scotland

Duncan, the king of Scotland, is the father of Malcolm and Donalbain. Duncan is also a cousin to Macbeth and is eventually murdered by him for the crown. Everyone, including Macbeth, regards Duncan as a good king. Macbeth observes that "this Duncan / Hath borne his faculties so meek, hath been / So clear in his great office, that his virtues / Will plead like angels." [90]

Duncan rewards Macbeth with the thaneship of Cawdor for his part in the defeat of Macdonwald and the Norwegians, but he names his son Malcolm as the heir to the Scottish throne. This thwarts Macbeth's hopes of becoming the king of Scotland (and the Weird Sisters' prediction). Desperate, Macbeth invites Duncan to his castle and murders him as he sleeps. Without the murder of the good and gentle King Duncan, Macbeth never would have had the chance to become king. Also, the fact that Macbeth kills Duncan as he sleeps under Macbeth's own roof illustrates the warping effect that ambition has had on Macbeth's character.

Fleance

Fleance is Banquo's son and only appears in a couple of the play's scenes. However, Fleance's small role is important because his mere existence means that Macbeth has doomed his soul for nothing: Fleance's sons will become kings of Scotland. The Weird

Sisters had predicted that the descendants of Banquo would take the throne from Macbeth, so Macbeth gives Banquo's assassins special instructions to kill Fleance as well. When the murderers report that Fleance has escaped, Macbeth realizes his future doom: "There the grown serpent lies; the worm that's fled / Hath nature that in time will venom breed, / No teeth for th' present."[91]

Gentlewoman

The gentlewoman plays a minor role in *Macbeth*. She is a servant to Lady Macbeth and a witness to Lady Macbeth's nocturnal wanderings. The gentlewoman, worried about Lady Macbeth's health, summons the Scots doctor to observe Lady Macbeth's sleepwalking and her confession about the murder of Duncan. After her appearance in act 5, scene 1 the gentlewoman does not appear in the rest of the play.

Lady Macbeth

Lady Macbeth is the ambitious wife of Macbeth and, as one critic has put it, "a woman who rages constantly against the limitations of her own sex."[92] In the first half of the play, Lady Macbeth leads and Macbeth follows. When she learns of the Weird Sisters' predictions, she is overjoyed because she wants to be queen, but worries that Macbeth "is too full o' th' milk of human kindness" to do what it takes to steal the crown from King Duncan. When she learns that Duncan will spend the night under her roof, Lady Macbeth invokes the spirits to "unsex" her and to fill her "from the crown to the toe topful / Of the direst cruelty"[93] so that she can murder Duncan herself.

Lady Macbeth also coaches an undecided Macbeth about how to act in the presence of the other nobles, and when he loses his resolve to commit the murder, Lady Macbeth questions his bravery, his love for her, and his manhood. She finally tells Macbeth that if she had made a promise such as he made to her, she would have plucked her nipple from the mouth of her baby "and dash'd the brains out."[94] Lady Macbeth then outlines for Macbeth how they will go about killing King Duncan, and Macbeth is so shocked by his wife's cold-bloodedness that he tells her "bring forth men-children only!"[95]

Critic Victor L. Cahn has speculated that since Lady Macbeth is childless, "then her desperation for worldly power is compensation for her failure in what was in Shakespeare's day regarded as

Lady Macbeth, the ambitious wife of Macbeth, wants to be queen of Scotland.

woman's essential role: motherhood."[96] Whatever the cause of Lady Macbeth's ambition, she ultimately succumbs to the guilt that she feels over Duncan's murder. The last part of the play finds her sleepwalking, trying to wash Duncan's blood from her hands, and reliving the night of the murder. Lady Macbeth, wracked by guilt, commits suicide in act 5, scene 5. Her death hardly moves Macbeth at all.

The purpose of Lady Macbeth's character is to demonstrate Macbeth's lack of resolve at the beginning of the play. Whenever Macbeth's resolve to kill Duncan wavers, Lady Macbeth encourages him to follow through with the plan. The audience realizes that without her insistence Macbeth probably would not have killed Duncan. Thus, Macbeth would not have murdered the others.

Lennox

Lennox is one of the Scottish lords who attends King Duncan. After Duncan's murder, Lennox enters the chamber with Macbeth, and he describes how they found the drunken chamberlains splattered with blood and sleeping. Lennox then describes how Macbeth killed the chamberlains in a fit of rage, an act that Lennox seems to condone. After the death of Banquo and Macbeth's strange behavior at the banquet, Lennox begins to suspect Macbeth of the murders of Duncan and Banquo, and he begins to sympathize with the exiled Malcolm and Macduff, even sending them greetings in act 3, scene 6. Lennox remains by Macbeth's side throughout the latter half of the play until act 5, scene 2, when he joins other Scottish lords in rebelling against Macbeth's rule.

Lennox is a minor character who reflects the type of person who changes loyalties as circumstances dictate. When Duncan is in power, Lennox is loyal to him, but when Macbeth is crowned king, Lennox shifts his allegiance to Macbeth even though he suspects him of murdering Duncan. Finally, when it is apparent that Malcolm will overthrow Macbeth, Lennox defects to Malcolm's side.

Macbeth

Of all of Shakespeare's tragic heros, Macbeth is the darkest. He is a cousin to King Duncan and a respected general in the Scottish army. At the beginning of the play Macbeth is an honorable man who is brave, eloquent, and energetic. However, after Macbeth hears the prophecies of the Weird Sisters, he is overwhelmed by ambition. Macbeth's tragic flaw is his unbridled ambition for the crown, which overrides his morals and drives him to murder Duncan, even though he realizes that such an act is wrong on many levels. Macbeth knows that "blood will have blood" and realizes that after Banquo's murder he is "in blood / Stepp'd in so far that, should I wade no more, / Returning were as tedious as go o'er." Macbeth decides to go ahead with his plan even though he knows that "things bad begun make strong themselves by ill."[97] Macbeth continues on his murderous course of action because he is determined to hold on to the crown.

With each murder, Macbeth's character becomes more brutal. However, he is also wracked by a guilt he cannot calm. The guilt he feels after murdering King Duncan manifests itself in Macbeth's insomnia, and after the murder of Banquo, a guilt-ridden Macbeth is confronted by Banquo's accusing ghost. Macbeth's guilt leads to a paranoia that causes him to see conspirators everywhere, even in women and children. In the end, the only way to rid Scotland of the cancerous Macbeth is for Macduff to kill him and present his head to the rightful king, Malcolm. Critic Frank Kermode has observed that Macbeth "is an Everyman; and for him as for all habitual sinners the guilt that is at first a matter of choice becomes . . . a matter of fate. His torments of conscience no longer come between the desire and the act. He loses his distinctive humanity."[98] The character of Macbeth demonstrates the effect of evil on men who decide to give in to their less reputable instincts.

Macduff

Macduff is the thane of Fife and the husband of Lady Macduff. He initially discovers King Duncan murdered in Macbeth's castle and immediately suspects Macbeth of the crime. Later, when Macbeth is crowned king of Scotland, Macduff refuses to attend the coronation, which displeases Macbeth. The Weird Sisters warn Macbeth against Macduff but reassure him that "none of woman born / Shall harm Macbeth"[99]; they withhold that Macduff was a caesarean birth (an operation whereby a fetus is removed through the walls of the abdomen and uterus).

After Macbeth learns that Macduff has left Scotland to seek Malcolm's aid in England, he orders the deaths of Lady Macduff and all of their children. Rosse carries the bad news to Macduff and Malcolm in England, and Macduff promises revenge against Macbeth. Macduff and Malcolm lead an army of Scottish rebels and English soldiers against Macbeth at Dunsinane, where Macbeth and Macduff meet on the battlefield. Macbeth warns Macduff that he is charmed and that no man born from a woman shall harm him; Macduff, however, reveals that he was ripped from his mother's womb. Macduff kills Macbeth and then presents the tyrant's head to Malcolm. Macduff's character is meant to contrast with Macbeth: Whereas Macbeth commits regicide for personal reasons, Macduff commits regicide to protect the people from Macbeth.

Malcolm

Malcolm is the eldest son of King Duncan and the heir to the Scottish throne. He is also a second cousin to Macbeth. After Duncan's murder, Malcolm, fearing for his life, flees to England and the protection of King Edward. Macbeth uses Malcolm's flight to accuse him of arranging the murder of King Duncan, and Malcolm does appear suspicious for a while. Despite this, Macduff decides to visit Malcolm at the English court to try to recruit him to help overthrow Macbeth. At first Malcolm is suspicious of Macduff's motives for the visit. He wonders if Macduff is there to betray Malcolm to Macbeth or, if Macduff is there to betray Macbeth to Malcolm? Malcolm then tells Macduff that he agrees that "our country sinks beneath the yoke; / It weeps, it bleeds, and each new day a gash / Is added to her wounds," but he protests that Scotland is better off under Macbeth and admits that he would be a worse tyrant. Malcolm then convinces Macduff that he is a lustful and greedy man who possesses none of the "king-becoming graces."[100]

This is too much for Macduff, who begins to mourn for his country, and Malcolm, seeing Macduff's honesty, reveals that he was testing Macduff and that he is not a lustful or greedy man. The two men then organize the English army to march against Macbeth. At Birnan Wood, Malcolm orders his men to cut branches from the trees to conceal their movement toward Macbeth's stronghold on Dunsinane Hill, thus fulfilling one of the Weird Sisters' predictions. After the battle, Macduff presents Malcolm with Macbeth's head and proclaims Malcolm the rightful king of Scotland. Malcolm's assumption of the throne represents the return of the natural order of things, according to the Chain of Being, and the end of evil.

The Murderers

The murderers play minor, but important roles in *Macbeth*. The murderers act as Macbeth's evil servants and kill Banquo. It is unclear from the text of the play what type of misfortune has befallen them, but Macbeth manages to convince them that Banquo is the source of their adversity. When the murderers ambush Banquo, they kill him but they allow his son, Fleance, to escape. They report this news to Macbeth who is happy to hear of Banquo's death, but disappointed at Fleance's escape. It is also not clear from the text if the murderers who kill Banquo are the same ones who kill Macduff's wife and children later in the play. In some productions of the play, the murderers are the same, but in other productions the murderers of Macduff's wife and children are different from Banquo's murderers.

The Porter

The porter of Macbeth's castle serves a dual purpose in the play. On the one hand, he provides a bit of comic relief between two emotionally intense scenes—the murder of Duncan and the discovery of the crime. On the other hand, the porter reminds the audience that Macbeth has just turned his castle, and his life, into a living hell. In a soliloquy, the porter describes three types of sinners entering hell: a farmer who expected a higher price for his crop than he received, an equivocator, and a tailor who steals from his customer. All three apply to Macbeth because all three crimes are rooted in ambition.

After admitting Macduff and Lennox to the castle, the porter jests about drinking and lechery: "It provokes the desire, but it takes away the performance. Therefore, much drink may be said to be an equivocator with lechery."[101] One critic has observed, "The addictive powers of drink and lechery as described . . . may be likened to the role of ambition in Macbeth's life. It has inspired him to action, but also trapped him in perpetual hell."[102]

Rosse

Rosse, a Scottish nobleman, is one of the minor characters of the play who helps move the action to its dramatic conclusion. He is essentially a messenger who relates messages or happenings between characters. Rosse first appears in act 1, scene 2 bearing the news that Macbeth and Banquo had defeated the rebel Macdonwald and his Norwegian allies. King Duncan then commands Rosse to go to Macbeth, convey the king's pleasure, and usher Macbeth to the royal presence.

Later in the play, after the murder of Duncan, Rosse relates the strange occurrences since Duncan's death to an old man. Although Rosse suspects Macbeth of some complicity surrounding the death of Duncan, he resolves to go to Macbeth's coronation to show his respect. After Macbeth's bizarre behavior at the feast, Rosse is convinced of Macbeth's guilt and warns Lady Macduff to flee before Macbeth's assassins find her. Rosse then escapes to England, where he informs Macduff that his wife and children have been killed at Macbeth's command. Rosse then joins Macduff, Malcolm, and the English army in overthrowing Macbeth.

The Scots Doctor

The Scots Doctor is yet another minor character. He only appears in the last act of the play and witnesses Lady Macbeth's nocturnal hand-washing and reliving of the crime. Later, when Macbeth asks the doctor for his diagnosis of Lady Macbeth, the doctor correctly states that she is "not so sick . . . / As troubled with thick-coming fancies, / That keep her from her rest" and that he cannot cure her because "the patient / Must minister to himself." A bit later in the same scene, the Scots Doctor gives voice to the sentiments many of Macbeth's retainers must hold: "Were I from Dunsinane away and clear, / Profit again should hardly draw me here."[103] Like many of Macbeth's fleeing retainers, the doctor also would like to escape the rule of Macbeth. The appearance of the Scots Doctor provides the dramatic framework in which the audience witnesses Lady Macbeth's psychological degeneration.

Siward

There are two Siwards in Macbeth: Siward, the Earl of Northumberland who is the general of the English forces, and Young Siward who is his son. Old Siward helps Malcolm regain the throne of Scotland by assisting the rebel Scots in overthrowing Macbeth. Young Siward is old Siward's son and is killed by Macbeth in the course of the battle.

The Weird Sisters

The mysterious Weird Sisters play an important role in *Macbeth*. It is unclear where the Weird Sisters come from (and even if they are really women), but it is clear that they are witches in the service of the devil Hecat. The Weird Sisters primarily interact with Macbeth and encourage him in his murderous endeavors, but their encouragement affects all of the play's characters. The dramatic purpose of the Weird Sisters is to tempt Macbeth to his doom with half-truths, a task they successfully complete. However, scholars argue about the sisters' motives. Cahn sums it up best when he states, "These three figures are best viewed as invidious meddlers, toying

Through half truths, the Weird Sisters encourage Macbeth in his murderous endeavors.

with human action. The outcome of events matters little to them. They desire only to play upon human vulnerabilities, to tap the evil within, and they have chosen as the subject Macbeth, whose frailties and vices are exploitable."[104] Critics have debated the role of the Weird Sisters in the play for centuries: Do the Weird Sisters, through magic, control Macbeth and drive him to his downfall? Or, do the sisters only mislead Macbeth, which would mean that he is solely responsible for his actions?

CHAPTER FIVE

A Literary
Analysis of
Macbeth

L ike all of Shakespeare's plays, *Macbeth* has been the subject of scrutiny and criticism over the years. The volume
of *Macbeth* criticism and scholarship is far too vast to be
repeated in any detail here, but most of it can be grouped under
four questions: Is Macbeth a true tragic hero? What role does fate
play in *Macbeth*? What is Shakespeare trying to say about ambition? What message is Shakespeare attempting to send about
social stratification, especially in relation to the Chain of Being? By
examining these questions, critics hope to develop a deeper understanding of the play's characters and central themes.

Is Macbeth a True Tragic Hero?

When analyzing Shakespeare's plays, critic and author Samuel
Johnson observes that "Shakespeare has no heroes,"[105] meaning
that all of Shakespeare's characters are flawed in some respect.
Nowhere is that more true than in *Macbeth*. However, *Macbeth* is
a tragedy, and all tragedies must have a tragic hero. *Macbeth*'s
tragic hero is the character of Macbeth. The question "Is Macbeth
a true tragic hero?" has often been debated by critics. The classical concept of the tragedy and the tragic hero demands that a
tragedy involve a noble character of flawless morals, except for a

single "tragic flaw" such as greed, ambition, optimism, or jeal-ousy. A tragic hero chooses to indulge his tragic flaw, fully aware of the consequences of his choice, and thereby damns himself.

The argument has often been made that Macbeth is not a true tragic hero, but rather the pawn of supernatural forces. Some critics, such as Victor L. Cahn, "believe that the witches ordain their subsequent meetings with Macbeth and that they determine his future. According to this interpretation the play is about fate, and in murdering Duncan, Macbeth is only playing out his des-tiny." [106] True, the Weird Sisters do choose Macbeth for unknown reasons, and they do predict that he will become the thane of Cawdor and the king of Scotland. The argument has even been made that when the Weird Sisters hex Macbeth in act 1, scene 3 and act 4, scene 1 they are taking the decision out of Macbeth's hands. Indeed, scholars have traced the origin of the sisters' name: *Weird* is derived from the Old English word *wyrd*, which meant "fate."

Other scholars argue that Macbeth is not a tragic hero because he has substantial help with Duncan's murder from his wife. Some scholars believe that Lady Macbeth deserves part of the credit for Macbeth's downfall because she encourages him in his murderous endeavor and goes so far as to come up with the plan for Duncan's murder. Gareth Lloyd Evans points out that "the Macbeth we meet before he rejoins his wife is, basically, a morally weak man. . . . He has little will-power over his baser instincts." [107] However, he has not yet made up his mind about the killing. But, as soon as Macbeth comes in contact with Lady Macbeth, she makes up his mind for him through manipulations and insults. Indeed, when Macbeth falters during the murder of Duncan, Lady Macbeth is the one who takes the daggers back to the scene of the crime and smears the chamberlains with blood.

Nevertheless, plenty of evidence supports the idea that Macbeth is a true tragic hero. His tragic flaw is his unbridled lust for power coupled with a propensity for violence. After the Weird Sisters foretell his thaneship of Cawdor and his kingship of

Since Lady Macbeth came up with the plan to kill Duncan, some scholars argue that she bears some of the responsibility for Macbeth's downfall.

Scotland, and after half of the prophecy is confirmed by Rosse, Macbeth immediately begins to entertain the notion of murdering Duncan. Later, when the king names Malcolm as his heir, Macbeth begins to reconcile himself to the murder plot. Once Macbeth has the crown, his desire to hold on to power leads him to commit a series of increasingly brutal crimes.

True, Macbeth is encouraged by the Weird Sisters, but it is Macbeth himself who decides to make the predictions come

true by murdering Duncan. Macbeth is foolish to believe anything the Weird Sisters tell him, and Banquo even warns him
against them. The Weird Sisters do seem to have some control
over the environment, such as killing animals, controlling the
weather, and conjuring greater demons, but the play does not
make clear the extent of their power. The Weird Sisters egg on
Macbeth, but ultimately it is Macbeth who decides what his
destiny will be.

Even though Lady Macbeth helps her husband by planning
the murder of Duncan and by aiding in the coverup of the crime,
she fails miserably as an accomplice at the end. It is Macbeth's
idea to murder Banquo and destroy Macduff's family, and Lady
Macbeth has no role in the conception or execution of these
crimes. Despite her request that she be filled from "crown to the
toe topful / Of direst cruelty,"[108] she abandons Macbeth when he
needs her most. It is Macbeth alone, encouraged by his wife and
the Weird Sisters, who is responsible for the deeds that eventually cause his downfall. Macbeth fully realizes the consequences of
his actions and also that "even-handed justice / Commends th'
ingredience of our poison'd chalice / to our own lips." In spite
of the consequences, Macbeth decides that it is worth putting
"rancors in the vessel of my peace . . . mine eternal jewel"[109] to
have the crown of Scotland. It is this conscious decision to sacri-
fice his soul for Scotland that makes Macbeth a true tragic hero;
he realizes what the consequences of his actions will be but insists
on pursuing them anyway.

A Question of Fate

The role of fate (or fortune) in *Macbeth* has been hotly debated
for centuries. Some critics contend that Macbeth has no control
over his destiny and is doomed from the start; other scholars
argue that Macbeth is free to make decisions, but he always makes
the wrong choices. According to medieval belief, mankind was
subject to Fate because the original sin of Adam and Eve had
placed humans below the stars and planets on the Chain of Being.

Thus, humans were subject to the unpredictable actions of the universe. Fate was usually represented as a wheel to symbolize its cyclical nature: One's fortune continually rises and falls like the turning of a wheel.

Scholars believe that Shakespeare is illustrating this concept in *Macbeth* with the Weird Sisters. Indeed, there is some evidence of this interpretation because the word *weird* in Elizabethan England still retained its Old English meaning of "fate," but it also carried the new connotation of "eerie or uncanny." During this time period, it was believed that the mechanism of fate was unknowable, that is, it was impossible to know one's destiny as well as change it. However, the reason the Weird Sisters choose Macbeth is unclear and leads one to believe that they are supposed to approach him because it is his destiny. Additionally, *Macbeth* illustrates the medieval concept of fate: It raises Macbeth to a high place only to bring him down again.

However, this explanation of the role of fate in *Macbeth* is based on a medieval concept and ignores the Renaissance idea of fate. The respected Renaissance scholar E. M. W. Tillyard notes that Elizabethans believed that "it was not primarily God who allowed it [evil] but man who inflicted it on both himself and the physical universe" and that "the general contention is that man has it in him to survive the blows of fortune [fate] and that ultimately fortune herself is . . . the tool of God and the educator of man. The good man ultimately is always happy, the bad man most unhappy when most successful in his evil plans."[110]

Accordingly, although the Weird Sisters predict that Macbeth will become king of Scotland, he is the one who ultimately decides to fulfill the prediction through murder. Frank Kermode writes, "The Weird Sisters, knowing of his ambitions, could persuade Macbeth to evil, but they could not compel him to it,"[111] an idea with which Elizabethan audiences would have been familiar. Ultimately, the Weird Sisters use their predictions to manipulate Macbeth into committing the evil actions that they cannot force him to exercise. However, in the end, it is Macbeth's choice not the Weird Sisters or fate that push Macbeth to murder Duncan, Banquo, and Macduff's wife and children.

The Chain of Being

Another Renaissance idea that influenced *Macbeth* was the Chain of Being, a concept central to understanding the dramatic intensity of the play. Tillyard once advanced the idea that to properly understand *Macbeth*, or any of Shakespeare's plays, it is necessary to understand the belief system in which they were created. The Renaissance idea of the Chain of Being defined the order of the entire universe and was widely assumed to be the "natural" order of things. According to this order, God was situated at the top since he was the supreme being. Below God were various ranks of angels and heavenly spirits, and below them, the highest humans, who were kings divinely appointed to their positions. Below the king were nobles, warriors, merchants, artisans, farmers, and peasants. Underneath humans on the Chain of Being came animals, vegetables, and minerals. Within each category, each person or object was ranked in relation to what came before it and what came after it. For example, gold was the best metal, followed by silver, with all the rest in order of their importance and/or value, with lead as the "basest" metal.

The Chain of Being was widely assumed by Elizabethans to be the "natural order" of the universe, and they attempted to imitate this order in their society. Renaissance English society was stratified to the extent that a person's social position dictated what clothes he or she could wear. This is why actors were viewed suspiciously: They wore the clothes of kings and queens (their social betters) and pretended to be nobles. Once again, Tillyard notes, "to us chaos means hardly more than confusion on a large scale; to an Elizabethan it meant the cosmic anarchy before creation and the wholesale dissolution that would result if the pressure of Providence relaxed and allowed the law of nature to cease functioning."[112] In other words if one link in the Chain of Being broke, moved, or ceased to exist, it would plunge the whole universe into disorder.

Even the most ignorant members of Shakespeare's audience would have been scandalized by Macbeth's murder of King Duncan and would have realized immediately the seriousness of his crime. Macbeth's act violates the Chain of Being in several ways. First and foremost, the king's body is holy and should not be violated. This is why Elizabethans considered regicide such a horrible crime. Also, regicides upset the "natural" balance by which God appoints kings. Secondly, Duncan is Macbeth's cousin and the Elizabethans considered the murder of family members especially horrendous. Additionally, Duncan is a guest in Macbeth's home, and it was traditionally believed that a host is supposed to protect his guest, not betray him.

Finally, Macbeth kills Duncan at Duncan's weakest moment: while he is sleeping. Because Macbeth violates nature and murders the King in his sleep—"the innocent sleep, / Sleep that knits up the ravell'd sleave of care, / The death of each day's life, sore labor's bath, / Balm of hurt minds, great nature's second course, / Chief nourisher in life's feast"—he is doomed to "sleep no more."[113] Later in the play, Macbeth complains that he would rather be dead than suffer "these terrible dreams / That shake us nightly."[114] In the last act of *Macbeth*, Lady Macbeth's sleepwalking betrays her to the Scots Doctor and the waiting gentlewoman. Sleep is an important link in the Chain of Being because it separates conscious living things (humans and animals) from nonliving things (trees and rocks). When Macbeth kills Duncan as he sleeps he violates the natural order of things and simultaneously lowers himself on the Chain of Being into a category of things which do not have a consciousness and do not sleep.

Throughout the play, Macbeth continues to violate the Chain of Being. He murders his friend Banquo and orders the murder of Macduff's wife and children. To Elizabethan audiences, Macbeth's violations of the Chain of Being would be seen as a threat to the foundations of civilization. Shakespeare, through the character of Macbeth, is attempting to illustrate the consequences of violating the natural order of the universe.

Shakespeare symbolizes this violation of the Chain of Being in several ways. After the murder of Duncan, the play becomes unnaturally dark. Indeed, the noted Shakespearean A. L. Rowse has described *Macbeth* as "a dark and sinister opera."[115] A. C. Bradley has remarked that "darkness, we may even say blackness, broods over this tragedy. It is remarkable that almost all the scenes which at once recur to memory take place either at night or in some dark spot."[116] In act 2, scene 4 Rosse comments to an old man about the unnatural darkness, even in daylight, that has fallen across Scotland since the murder of Duncan. This darkness symbolizes the evil of Macbeth, the wickedness of his reign over Scotland, and the disruption of the Chain of Being.

In this same scene, Rosse and the old man trade stories about the unusual behavior of animals that they have witnessed. The old man explains how he has seen a falcon killed by an owl. This is unusual because it violates the Chain of Being: A noble bird of prey is killed by a common owl. Rosse describes how Duncan's horses have "turn'd wild in nature, broke their stalls, flung out, / contending 'gainst obedience, as they would make / War with mankind."[117] These events are important to the characters because they demonstrate that the law of nature has ceased to function and that something is wrong in the universe. Because Macbeth has tampered with one part of the Chain of Being—the king—he has thrown the whole system into chaos: The sun refuses to shine, the stars fail to show themselves, and animals behave unnaturally.

In *Macbeth*, time also ceases to operate normally. The murder of Duncan causes an eternal darkness to descend on the play so that all of the action seems to take place during one long, dark night. Macbeth laments that his wife should have died later because there would have been time to mourn her, Malcolm asserts that he will fix those things that "I shall find the time to,"[118] and Lady Macbeth advises Macbeth "to beguile the time."[119] The fact that time has ceased to function is further evidence that nature has been violated. The pace of *Macbeth* also gives the play the feeling of being rushed, as if nature itself cannot wait to dispose of Macbeth and restore order according to the Chain of Being. Indeed, after the death of Macbeth, the victorious Malcolm assures his followers that he will perform everything that is required "in measure, time, and place." [120]

The violation of the Chain of Being is also represented by the figures of the Weird Sisters. The sisters inhabit a place at the bottom of the Chain of Being and are roughly a step above Satan, who is at the very bottom. When Macbeth follows the advice of the Weird Sisters instead of Christian teaching, he is willfully perverting the will of God. The Weird Sisters are so alien that Banquo cannot tell if they are spirits or humans, male or female: "You should be women, / And yet your beards forbid me to interpret / That you are so." [121] The Weird Sisters' equivocations to Macbeth also violate the Chain of Being because of the way in which the Sisters abuse language by making predictions that seem to mean one thing but, in fact, mean something totally different. Overall, *Macbeth* is Shakespeare's attempt to demonstrate the power of the Chain of Being. Through the character of Macbeth, Shakespeare shows that violations of the chain result not only in personal disaster but in universal disaster as well.

The Role of Ambition in Macbeth

All tragic heros must have a tragic flaw, and Macbeth's is his overwhelming ambition. The prominence of ambition in *Macbeth* can be seen as a direct relationship to Shakespeare's times and the deeply conflicted attitudes of the period concerning ambition. During the English Renaissance, the growing middle class clamored for more political rights, and the idea of the common people ruling instead of being ruled terrified the nobility. The nobility saw these actions as overly ambitious and contrary to the long-established Chain of Being. The nobles believed that the middle class—the common people—lacked the honor and the loyalty to participate in government and that it was "above" their station in the Chain of Being.

In a sense, *Macbeth* and his wife symbolize the middle-class desire to be more than what they are (or are supposed to be). Macbeth's ambition is unchecked by both moral and legal considerations—he will stop at nothing to get what he desires. Additionally, the thing that he desires—the crown—is above his station in life, and to obtain that position of power would upset the balance of nature. Macbeth's unbridled ambition is the root of the play's evil because he is willing to throw the world into chaos in order to satisfy his personal desires.

However, *Macbeth* also portrays ambition in a positive light when it is tempered with honor and loyalty. Banquo, Macduff, and Malcolm exhibit ambition to a certain degree, but not to the extremes that drive Macbeth. For example, after the Weird Sisters tell Banquo that he will be the founder of a line of kings, he dreams of the opportunity but asks the "merciful powers, / Restrain in me the cursed thoughts that nature / Gives way to in repose."[122] Furthermore, unlike Macbeth, Banquo restrains his desire when Macbeth hints that Banquo would be rewarded for supporting him. Banquo responds that he would be happy to help Macbeth so long as he does not lose any honor by doing so.

Like Banquo, Macduff and Malcolm's ambitions are tempered by honor and loyalty. Macduff's ambition is to live in peace with his family in a kingdom where he does not have to fear the misrule of Macbeth; Malcolm's only ambition is to gain the position that was promised to him: the throne of Scotland. The ambition of these three characters is checked by their loyalty to the Chain of Being: Each of them desires things that they are entitled to possess.

Macbeth also illustrates how ambitions can shift with loyalties and opportunities. Rosse and Lennox are two characters whose loyalties shift to accommodate their ambitions. Their only ambition seems to be to remain in favor with whoever is in power. After Duncan is killed, both men switch their allegiance to Macbeth even though they seem to suspect him of the murder. Likewise, when it becomes clear that Malcolm is going to triumph over Macbeth, neither Lennox nor Rosse loses much time in joining Malcolm's army. *Macbeth* is the study of the role of ambition in the lives of men. Some men, such as Macbeth, will do anything to satisfy their ambition while other men, such as Banquo, are able to temper their ambition.

Macbeth's actions are motivated by his ambition.

William Shakespeare's *Macbeth* has been around for almost four hundred years, and in that time it has inspired many radically different ideas. However, four general themes have spurred the most research: Macbeth's fitness as a tragic hero, the role of fate, the role of ambition in the tragedy, and the degree to which the play was shaped by Shakespeare's contemporary society. More than any other play, *Macbeth* demonstrates how Shakespeare was a man of the English Renaissance, concerned with current events and attempting to capitalize on public sentiment. Modern audiences are fascinated with *Macbeth* as a study in evil and by the psychological portrayal of his guilt. However, *Macbeth* also illustrates the mature powers of a skilled poet, dramatist, and student of human nature.

Notes

Chapter 1: The Life of William Shakespeare

1. Quoted in G. Blakemore Evans, ed., *The Riverside Shakespeare*. Boston: Houghton Mifflin, 1974, p. 1,069.

2. Quoted in Evans, *The Riverside Shakespeare*, p. 127.

3. Quoted in M. H. Abrams, ed., *The Norton Anthology of English Literature*, vol. 1, 6th ed. New York: W. W. Norton, 1993, p. 1,242.

4. Quoted in Edmund Chambers, *A Short Life of Shakespeare with the Sources*, ed. Charles Williams. London: Oxford University Press, 1963, p. 14.

5. Quoted in S. Schoenbaum, *William Shakespeare: A Compact Documentary Life*. New York: Oxford University Press, 1987, p. 73.

6. Quoted in Evans, *The Riverside Shakespeare*, p. 230.

7. Quoted in Evans, *The Riverside Shakespeare*, p. 1,069.

8. Quoted in Evans, *The Riverside Shakespeare*, p. 117.

9. Quoted in Levi Fox, *The Shakespeare Handbook*. Boston: G. K. Hall, 1987, p. 92.

10. Quoted in Evans, *The Riverside Shakespeare*, p. 1,835.

11. Quoted in Schoenbaum, *William Shakespeare*, p. 176.

12. Quoted in Evans, *The Riverside Shakespeare*, p. 1,705.

13. Nicholas Rowe, "Some Acount of the Life &c. of Mr. William Shakespear," Mr. William Shakespeare and the Internet. http://shakespeare.palomar.edu/rowe.htm.

14. Quoted in Schoenbaum, *William Shakespeare*, p. 249.

15. Quoted in James Joyce, *Ulysses*. New York: Random Books, 1914, p. 263.

Chapter 2: The History of *Macbeth*

16. Bruce Heydt, "Fair and Foul Macbeth," *British Heritage*, June/July 2000, p. 56.

17. Heydt, "Fair and Foul Macbeth," p. 57.

18. Heydt, "Fair and Foul Macbeth," p. 57.

19. Heydt, "Fair and Foul Macbeth," p. 57.

20. Quoted in Evans, *The Riverside Shakespeare*, p. 1,330.

21. Quoted in Evans, *The Riverside Shakespeare*, p. 1,339.

22. Quoted in F. E. Halliday, ed., *Shakespeare and His Critics*. New York: Schocken Books, 1963, p. 258.

23. Quoted in Halliday, *Shakespeare and His Critics*, p. 258.

24. Quoted in Halliday, *Shakespeare and His Critics*, p. 258.

25. Quoted in Evans, *The Riverside Shakespeare*, p. 1,848.

Chapter 3: The Plot of *Macbeth:* A Study of Evil

26. Quoted in Evans, *The Riverside Shakespeare*, p. 1,307.

27. Quoted in Evans, *The Riverside Shakespeare*, p. 1,312.

28. Quoted in Evans, *The Riverside Shakespeare*, p. 1,314.

29. Quoted in Evans, *The Riverside Shakespeare*, p. 1,314.

30. Quoted in Evans, *The Riverside Shakespeare*, p. 1,314.

31. Quoted in Evans, *The Riverside Shakespeare*, p. 1,314.

32. Quoted in Evans, *The Riverside Shakespeare*, p. 1,315.

33. Quoted in Evans, *The Riverside Shakespeare*, p. 1,316.

34. Quoted in Evans, *The Riverside Shakespeare*, p. 1,317.

35. Quoted in Evans, *The Riverside Shakespeare*, p. 1,317.

36. Quoted in Evans, *The Riverside Shakespeare*, p. 1,318.

37. Quoted in Evans, *The Riverside Shakespeare*, p. 1,318.

38. Quoted in Evans, *The Riverside Shakespeare*, p. 1,318.

39. Quoted in Evans, *The Riverside Shakespeare*, p. 1,319.

40. Quoted in Evans, *The Riverside Shakespeare*, pp. 1,319, 1,320.

41. Quoted in Evans, *The Riverside Shakespeare*, p. 1,320.

42. Quoted in Evans, *The Riverside Shakespeare*, p. 1,321.

43. Quoted in Evans, *The Riverside Shakespeare*, p. 1,321.

44. Quoted in Evans, *The Riverside Shakespeare*, p. 1,322.

45. Quoted in Evans, *The Riverside Shakespeare*, p. 1,322.

46. Quoted in Evans, *The Riverside Shakespeare*, p. 1,322.

47. Quoted in Evans, *The Riverside Shakespeare*, p. 1,322.

48. Quoted in Evans, *The Riverside Shakespeare*, p. 1,323.

49. Quoted in Evans, *The Riverside Shakespeare*, p. 1,323.

50. Quoted in Evans, *The Riverside Shakespeare*, p. 1,324.

51. Quoted in Evans, *The Riverside Shakespeare*, p. 1,324.

52. Quoted in Evans, *The Riverside Shakespeare*, p. 1,325.

53. Quoted in Evans, *The Riverside Shakespeare*, p. 1,325.

54. Quoted in Evans, *The Riverside Shakespeare*, p. 1,325.

55. Quoted in Evans, *The Riverside Shakespeare*, p. 1,325.

56. Quoted in Evans, *The Riverside Shakespeare*, p. 1,326.

57. Quoted in Evans, *The Riverside Shakespeare*, p. 1,326.

58. Quoted in Evans, *The Riverside Shakespeare*, p. 1,326.

59. Quoted in Evans, *The Riverside Shakespeare*, p. 1,326.

60. Quoted in Evans, *The Riverside Shakespeare*, p. 1,327.

61. Quoted in Evans, *The Riverside Shakespeare*, p. 1,327.

62. Quoted in Evans, *The Riverside Shakespeare*, p. 1,329.

63. Quoted in Evans, *The Riverside Shakespeare*, p. 1,329.

64. Quoted in Evans, *The Riverside Shakespeare*, p. 1,329.

65. Quoted in Evans, *The Riverside Shakespeare*, p. 1,330.

66. Quoted in Evans, *The Riverside Shakespeare*, p. 1,331.

67. Quoted in Evans, *The Riverside Shakespeare*, p. 1,331.

68. Quoted in Evans, *The Riverside Shakespeare*, p. 1,331.

69. Quoted in Evans, *The Riverside Shakespeare*, p. 1,332.

70. Quoted in Evans, *The Riverside Shakespeare*, p. 1,333.

71. Quoted in Evans, *The Riverside Shakespeare*, p. 1,334.

72. Quoted in Evans, *The Riverside Shakespeare*, p. 1,335.

73. Quoted in Evans, *The Riverside Shakespeare*, p. 1,335.

74. Quoted in Evans, *The Riverside Shakespeare*, p. 1,335.

75. Quoted in Evans, *The Riverside Shakespeare*, p. 1,336.

76. Quoted in Evans, *The Riverside Shakespeare*, p. 1,336.

77. Quoted in Evans, *The Riverside Shakespeare*, p. 1,336.

78. Quoted in Evans, *The Riverside Shakespeare*, p. 1,337.

79. Quoted in Evans, *The Riverside Shakespeare*, p. 1,337.

80. Quoted in Evans, *The Riverside Shakespeare*, p. 1,338.

81. Quoted in Evans, *The Riverside Shakespeare*, p. 1,338.

82. Quoted in Evans, *The Riverside Shakespeare*, p. 1,338.

83. Quoted in Evans, *The Riverside Shakespeare*, pp. 1,338–39.

84. Quoted in Evans, *The Riverside Shakespeare*, p. 1,339.

85. Quoted in Evans, *The Riverside Shakespeare*, p. 1,339.

Chapter 4: The Characters of *Macbeth*

86. Quoted in Evans, *The Riverside Shakespeare*, p. 1,314.

87. Quoted in Evans, *The Riverside Shakespeare*, p. 1,323.

88. Victor L. Cahn, *Shakespeare the Playwright*. New York: Greenwood, 1991, p. 190.

89. Quoted in Evans, *The Riverside Shakespeare*, p. 1,322.

90. Quoted in Evans, *The Riverside Shakespeare*, p. 1,317.

91. Quoted in Evans, *The Riverside Shakespeare*, p. 1,326.

92. Peter Quennell and Hamish Johnson, *Who's Who in Shakespeare*. New York: Oxford University Press, 1995, p. 134.

93. Quoted in Evans, *The Riverside Shakespeare*, p. 1,316.

94. Quoted in Evans, *The Riverside Shakespeare*, p. 1,318.

95. Quoted in Evans, *The Riverside Shakespeare*, p. 1,318.

96. Cahn, *Shakespeare the Playwright*, p.189.

97. Quoted in Evans, *The Riverside Shakespeare*, pp. 1,327, 1,325.

98. Quoted in Evans, *The Riverside Shakespeare*, p. 1,309.

99. Quoted in Evans, *The Riverside Shakespeare*, p. 1,329.

100. Quoted in Evans, *The Riverside Shakespeare*, pp. 1,332, 1,333.

101. Quoted in Evans, *The Riverside Shakespeare*, p. 1,320.

102. Cahn, *Shakespeare the Playwright*, p. 193.

103. Quoted in Evans, *The Riverside Shakespeare*, pp. 1,336, 1,337.

104. Cahn, *Shakespeare the Playwright*, p. 181.

Chapter 5: A Literary Analysis of *Macbeth*

105. Quoted in Abrams, *The Norton Anthology of Literature*, p. 2,395.

106. Cahn, *Shakespeare the Playwright*, p. 180.

107. Gareth Lloyd Evans, *The Upstart Crow: An Introduction to Shakespeare's Plays*. London: J. M. Dent and Sons, 1982, p. 296.

108. Quoted in Evans, *The Riverside Shakespeare*, p. 1,315.

109. Quoted in Evans, *The Riverside Shakespeare*, pp. 1,317, 1,323.

110. E. M. W. Tillyard, *The Elizabethan World Picture*. New York: Vintage Books, 1942, pp. 54, 56.

111. Quoted in Evans, *The Riverside Shakespeare*, p. 1,309.

112. Tillyard, *The Elizabethan World Picture*, p. 16.

113. Quoted in Evans, *The Riverside Shakespeare*, p. 1,320.

114. Quoted in Evans, *The Riverside Shakespeare*, p. 1,325.

115. A. L. Rowse, *Shakespeare the Man*. New York: St. Martin's, 1988, p. 190.

116. Quoted in Halliday, *Shakespeare and His Critics*, p. 262.

117. Quoted in Evans, *The Riverside Shakespeare*, p. 1,322.

118. Quoted in Evans, *The Riverside Shakespeare*, p. 1,332.

119. Quoted in Evans, *The Riverside Shakespeare*, p. 1,317.

120. Quoted in Evans, *The Riverside Shakespeare*, p. 1,339.

121. Quoted in Evans, *The Riverside Shakespeare*, p. 1,314.

122. Quoted in Evans, *The Riverside Shakespeare*, p. 1,318.

For Further Exploration

Below are some suggestions for potential essays on *Macbeth*.

1. *Macbeth* has been called Shakespeare's darkest play in terms of its setting, tone, characters, and theme. Review the play and determine which of these four elements is most responsible for the play's "darkness" and explain why. *See* William Hazlitt, *In Praise of Macbeth*; A. C. Bradley, *The Tone of Macbeth*.

2. According to Renaissance belief, fate determined the outcome of situations and humans had little control over their own lives. Many scholars have criticized *Macbeth* as a tragedy because they claim that Macbeth's actions are predetermined and that he has little choice but to follow the predictions of the Weird Sisters. Do you agree or disagree with this idea? Specifically, what in the play supports your position? *See:* Charles Lamb, *Thoughts on the Weird Sisters*; Robert Ornstein, *Macbeth's Motives*.

3. Compare and contrast the characters of Macbeth, Banquo, and Macduff. How are the three men similar? How are they different? What do you think they are supposed to symbolize? Refer to specific passages in the play to support your ideas.

4. In what ways does Macbeth's murder of Duncan and his subsequent reign as king affect the natural world and the kingdom of Scotland in particular? Why do you think Shakespeare included these details? Make your answers as specific as possible.

5. Think about Lady Macbeth. How is she similar to her husband? How is she different from him? What is her role in the play? Why do you think Shakespeare included her? *See* Edith Sitwell, *The Three Tragic Themes of Macbeth*; G. Wilson Knight, *"Macbeth" and "Antony and Cleopatra."*

6. The Weird Sisters and the ghost of Banquo play minor but important roles in *Macbeth*. However, some critics claim that the sisters and the ghost do not really exist but are figments of Macbeth's mind. Do you believe this assertion is true? Why or why not? Use specific instances from the play to support your position.

7. *Equivocation* is defined in the dictionary as "the use of ambiguous expressions especially in order to mislead" and "to deliberately misstate or create an incorrect impression." With this definition in mind, reread the Weird Sisters' predictions (act 1, scene 3, lines 48–50 and 65–68; act 4, scene 1, lines 71–72, 79–81, and 90–94). How do each of these predictions mislead Macbeth?

8. Macbeth's actions in the first part of the play are treacherous and murderous, yet audiences tend to identify and sympathize with him. However, by the end of the play audiences want Macbeth punished for his actions. At what specific point in the play does Macbeth lose the sympathy of the audience? What is it about this event that changes the audience's opinion of his character? *See* Gareth Lloyd Evans, *The Strange Power of Macbeth;* Robert Ornstein, *Macbeth's Motives.*

9. Some feminists have criticized Shakespeare because they say his female characters are stereotypical and shallow. Think about the women in *Macbeth*. Which characters are female? How would you describe these characters? What, if any, stereotypes do these characters fit? Do you believe Shakespeare is a sexist? Why or why not? Be specific. *See* Charles Lamb, *Thoughts on the Weird Sisters;* Edith Sitwell, *The Three Tragic Themes of Macbeth;* G. Wilson Knight, *"Macbeth" and "Antony and Cleopatra."*

10. By definition, a tragedy is "a dramatic composition dealing with a serious theme, typically that of a noble person whose character is flawed by a single weakness, such as pride or envy, which causes him to break a divine law or moral precept and which inevitably leads to his downfall or destruction." Describe Macbeth's tragic flaw. How does this lead to his downfall? What divine law(s) and/or moral precept(s) does Macbeth violate? What is the moral of *Macbeth?* *See* William Hazlitt, *In Praise of Macbeth;* Robert Ornstein, *Macbeth's Motives.*

11. At the end of act 1, scene 1 the Weird Sisters introduce the paradoxical idea that "Fair is foul, and foul is fair." What does this phrase mean? Specifically, how is this idea realized in *Macbeth?*

Appendix of Criticism

The First Record of *Macbeth*

In Mackbeth at the glod [Globe] 1610 [1611] the 20 of Aprill [Saturday]. ther was to be [observed] firste howe Mackbeth and Bancko 2 noble [men] of Scotland Ridinge thorowe a wod [wood] [there] stode befor them 3 women feiries or Nimphes And Saluted Mackbeth saying .t. 3 tymes unto him. haille mackbeth. king of Codon for thou shalt be a kinge.

> Simon Forman, "Contemporary Notices of Plays and Poems," in *The Riverside Shakespeare*, ed. G. Blakemore Evans. Boston: Houghton Mifflin, 1974, p. 1,841.

Early Praise for Shakespeare's *Macbeth*

December 28, 1666: To the Duke's House, and there saw *Macbeth* most excellently acted and a most excellent play for variety.

January 7, 1667: To the Duke's House and saw *Macbeth*, which, though I saw it lately, yet appears a most excellent play in all respects, but especially in divertisement, though it be a deep tragedy; which is a strange perfection in a tragedy, it being most proper here, and suitable.

April 19, 1667: to the play-house, where saw *Macbeth*, which, though I have seen it often, yet is one of the best plays for a stage, and a variety of dancing and musick, that ever I saw.

> Samuel Pepys, "Macbeth," in F. E. Halliday, ed., *Shakespeare and His Critics*. New York: Schocken Books, 1963, p. 258.

John Dryden Criticizes Shakespeare's Difficult Language

Yet it must be allow'd to the present Age, that the tongue in general is so much more refin'd since Shakespear's time, that many of his words, and more of his Phrases, are scarce intelligible. And of those which we understand some are ungrammatical, others [coarse]; and his whole style is so pester'd with Figurative expressions, that it is as affected as it is obscure. . . . If Shakespear be allow'd, as I think he must, to have made his characters distinct, it will easily be infer'd that he understood the nature of the passions: because it has been prov'd already, that confus'd passions make undistinguishable characters: yet I cannot deny that he has his failings: but they are not so much in the passions themselves, as in his manner of expression: he often obscures his meaning by his words, and sometimes makes it unintelligible.

> John Dryden, in *The Riverside Shakespeare*, ed. G. Blakemore Evans. Boston: Houghton Mifflin, 1974, p. 1,848.

Samuel Johnson Praises Shakespeare

Shakespeare is, above all writers, at least above all modern writers, the poet of nature, the poet that holds up to his readers a faithful mirror of manners and of life. His characters are not modified by the customs of particular places, unpracticed by the rest of the world . . . they are the genuine progeny of common humanity, such as the world will always supply and observation will always find. His persons act and speak by the influence of those general passions and principles by which all minds are agitated and the whole system of life is continued in motion. In the writings of other poets a character is too often an individual; in those of Shakespeare it is commonly a species.

Samuel Johnson, in *The Norton Anthology of Literature*, ed. M. H. Abrams. New York: W. W. Norton, 1993, p. 2,394.

Samuel Johnson Points Out a Flaw in *Macbeth*

Macbeth proceeds to wish, in the madness of guilt, that the inspection of Heaven may be intercepted, and that he may, in the involutions of infernal darkness, escape the eye of Providence. This is the utmost extravagance of determined wickedness: yet this is so debased by two unfortunate words, that while I endeavour to impress on my reader the energy of the sentiment, I can scarcely check my risibility, when the expression forces itself upon my mind; for who, without some relaxation of his gravity, can hear of the avengers of guilt *peeping through a blanket?*

Samuel Johnson, in *Shakespeare and His Critics*, ed., F. E. Halliday. New York: Schocken Books, 1963, p. 259.

Thoughts on the Weird Sisters

These are creatures to whom man or woman plotting some dire mischief might resort for the occasional consultation. Those originate deeds of blood, and begin bad impulses to men. From the moment that their eyes first meet with Macbeth's, he is spellbound. That meeting sways his destiny. He can never break the fascination. . . . The hags of Shakespeare have neither child of their own, nor seem descended from any parent. They are foul anomalies, of whom we know not whence they are sprung, nor whether they have beginning or ending. As they are without human passions, so they seem to be without human relations. They come with thunder and lightning, and vanish to airy music. This is all we know of them. Except Hecate, they have no names; which heighten their mysteriousness.

Charles Lamb, in *Shakespeare and His Critics*, ed., F. E. Halliday. New York: Schocken Books, 1963, pp. 259–60.

In Praise of *Macbeth*

Macbeth (generally speaking) is done upon a stronger and more systematic principle of contrast than any other of Shakespeare's plays. It moves upon the verge of an abyss, and is a constant struggle between life and death. The action is desperate and the reaction is dreadful. It is a huddling together of fierce extremes, a war of opposite natures which of them shall destroy the other. There is nothing but what has a violent end or violent beginnings. The lights and shades are laid on with a determined hand; the transitions from triumph to despair, from the height of terror to the repose of death, are sudden and startling; every passion brings in its fellow-contrary, and the thoughts pitch and jostle against each other in the dark. The whole play is unruly chaos of strange and forbidden things, where the ground rocks under our feet. Shakespeare's genius here took its full swing, and trod upon the farthest bounds of nature and passion.

> William Hazlitt, in *Shakespeare and His Critics*, ed.,
> F. E. Halliday. New York: Schocken Books, 1963, pp. 260–61.

Coleridge Comments on the Language of *Macbeth*

Macbeth stands in contrast throughout with *Hamlet;* in the manner of the opening especially. . . . [In *Macbeth*] the invocation is at once made to the imagination and the emotions connected therewith. Hence the movement throughout is the most rapid of all Shakespeare's plays; and hence also, with the exception of the disgusting passage of the Porter which I dare pledge myself to demonstrate to be an interpolation of the actors, there is not, to the best of my remembrance, a single pun or play on words in the whole drama. . . . Macbeth's language is the grave utterance of the very heart, conscience-sick, even to the last faintings of moral death. It is the same in all the other characters. The variety arises from rage, caused ever and anon by disruption of anxious thought, and the quick transition of fear into it.

> Samuel Coleridge, in *Shakespeare and His Critics*, ed.,
> F. E. Halliday. New York: Schocken Books, 1963, p. 261.

The Tone of *Macbeth*

A Shakespearean tragedy, as a rule, has a special tone of atmosphere of its own, quite perceptible, however difficult to describe. The effect of this atmosphere is marked with unusual strength in *Macbeth*. It is due to a variety of influences which combine with those just noticed, so that, acting and reacting, they form a whole; and the desolation of the blasted heath, the design of the Witches, the guilt in the hero's soul, the darkness of the night, seem to emanate from one and the same source. This effect is strengthened by a multitude of small touches, which at the moment may be little noticed but still leave their mark on the imagination. . . . All this has one effect, to excite the supernatural alarm and, even more, a dread of the presence of evil not only in its recognised seat but all through and around our mysterious nature. Perhaps there is no other work equal to *Macbeth* in the production of this effect.

> A. C. Bradley, in *Shakespeare and His Critics*, ed., F. E.
> Halliday. New York: Schocken Books, 1963, pp. 262–63.

The Three Tragic Themes of *Macbeth*

In this vast world torn from the universe of night, there are three tragic themes. The first theme is that of the actual guilt, and the separation in damnation of the two characters—the man who, in spite of his guilt, walks the road of the spirit, and who loves the light that has forsaken him—and the woman who, after her invocation to the "Spirits who tend on mortall thoughts," walks in the material world, and who does not know that light exists, until she is nearing her end. . . . The second tragic theme of the play is the man's love for the woman whose damnation is of the earth, who is unable, until death is near, to conceive of the damnation of the spirit, and who in her blindness therefore strays away from him, leaving him for ever in his lonely hell. . . . The third tragic theme is the woman's despairing love for the man whose vision she cannot see, and whom she has helped to drive into damnation.

> Edith Sitwell, in *Shakespeare and His Critics*, ed., F. E. Halliday, New York: Schocken Books, 1963, p. 263.

The Strange Power of *Macbeth*

Macbeth is Shakespeare's most haunting play. It not only stirs but frightens the imagination. It is also a "favourite" play of many readers and theatre-goers. There is a connection between what it does to the imagination and its attraction for it. There are certain places, certain books, certain pieces of music, certain pictures, certain people, which, when we meet or recall them, energize our emotions in a particular way, causing them to rise to the point almost beyond tolerance, and while we are caught within their power almost anything seems possible. *Macbeth*, especially when read, offers many moments when the play seems likely to leap from the page, embodying itself into some monstrous shape which will engulf the reader. Perhaps, indeed, the power of the play rests in its curious ability to make us believe, even in the reading, that it will come alive.

> Gareth Lloyd Evans, *The Upstart Crow: An Introduction to Shakespeare's Plays*. London: J. M. Dent and Sons, 1982, p. 293.

The Devil in *Macbeth*

[In *Macbeth*], the Third Murderer . . . is unidentified, and the First Murderer points out his strange entrance, raising a question of his origin that has long awaited a satisfactory answer. . . . Much critical discussion has focused on castings of the Third Murderer, which include Macbeth himself or, more plausibly, his terse companion Seyton. It is generally agreed that three murderers continue many other patterns of three in the play, all satanic perversions of the Trinity. Even if the "Seyton" homophone does not apply, these murderers are . . . devils.

> Michael Baird Saenger, "Shakespeare's *Macbeth*," *Explicator*, Spring 1995, p. 133.

Macbeth and *Antony and Cleopatra*

[*Macbeth* and *Antony and Cleopatra*] are clearly dominated by a woman. In no other play do we find just this relation existent between hero and heroine. Lady Macbeth and Cleopatra each possess a unique power and vitality which is irresistible and expressly feminine: their mastery is twined with their femininity. Each is very feminine: we might note that both faint at crucial moments. Each rules her man in somewhat similar fashion and with somewhat similar results. In Macbeth and Antony we find, too, a very definite masculine weakness and strength alternate. Both are fine warriors; both are plastic to their women. They fail in warriorship and practical affairs in proportion as they absorb and are absorbed by the more spiritual forces embodied in their women. Antony grows strong in love, Macbeth in evil.

G. Wilson Knight, in *Shakespeare: The Tragedies*, ed., Clifford Leech. Chicago: University of Chicago Press, 1965, p. 68.

Macbeth's Motives

A more conventional dramatist would have suggested that Macbeth piles murder on murder because his first act of blood brutalizes his nature. Shakespeare gives us a more terrible Macbeth who is driven to kill again and again because he cannot live with the memory of his first crime. Though the crime was perfect, neither he nor his wife was perfect in the crime. After the intoxicating rapture of murder wears off, she sinks into madness. Her diseased mind seeks to erase the horror of what she and Macbeth have done by rehearsing the murder scene over and over again in her dreams until the memory no longer tortures. Macbeth, more accustomed to killing and more capable of enduring blood, seeks to erase horror with horror. He will re-enact the crime again and again until his nature and his role are one, until he is "perfect" in his part, and a full feast of slaughter has blunted all moral sensitivity. As the recurrent imagery of drunkenness intimates, Macbeth's craving for blood is like a drunkard's thirst for oblivion, one that can bring no release because each satisfaction merely intensifies the original need, and the only oblivion can be bestiality itself.

Robert Ornstein, in *Shakespeare: The Tragedies*, ed., Clifford Leech. Chicago: University of Chicago Press, 1965, pp. 223–24.

Chronology

1558
The coronation of Queen Elizabeth.

1564
William Shakespeare is born on April 23 to John and Mary Shakespeare in Stratford-upon-Avon.

1570
Queen Elizabeth is excommunicated by Pope Pius V.

1573
Henry Wriothesley, earl of Southampton, is born; he will later become Shakespeare's patron.

1577
Sir Francis Drake begins his journey around the world; John Shakespeare's fortunes begin to decline, and he sinks into debt; William Shakespeare is withdrawn from school and probably becomes an apprentice in his father's shop.

1580
Drake returns from his voyage in triumph after attacking Spanish ships and capturing tremendous booty.

1582
William Shakespeare, age eighteen, marries Anne Hathaway, age twenty-six; she is already three months pregnant.

1583
Susanna, Shakespeare's first child, is baptized on May 26.

1584
Sir Walter Raleigh's expedition to inspect North America for colonization is a failure.

1585
English colonists are sent to Roanoke Island, Virginia, and disappear under mysterious circumstances; Hamnet and Judith, Shakespeare's twin son and daughter, are baptized on February 2; Shakespeare leaves Stratford for unknown reasons.

1587
Mary, Queen Elizabeth's Catholic half sister, is executed on the queen's order; Drake attacks and cripples the Spanish fleet at Cadiz.

[handwritten annotation: 1ST COUSIN, ONCE REMOVED]

1588
The Spanish Armada is defeated by the British navy; patriotic fervor is at an all-time high in England.

1589
Shakespeare's first play, *Henry VI*, Part 1, is written and performed to popular acclaim.

1591
Tea is first introduced into England.

1592
The bubonic plague strikes London, and the public theaters are closed; jealous about Shakespeare's success, Robert Greene attacks him in his *A Groatsworth of Wit* as an "upstart crow."

1593
Shakespeare dedicates "Venus and Adonis" to Henry Wriothesley, earl of Southampton, in an attempt to secure his patronage.

1594
Shakespeare dedicates "The Rape of Lucrece," the sequel to "Venus and Adonis," to the earl of Southampton; he begins writing the *Sonnets.*

1595
The plague eases, and London's public theaters reopen for business; Shakespeare becomes associated with the Lord Chamberlain's Men as a "sharer" (stockholder); he reportedly purchases his share with money given to him by Southampton.

1596
The Shakespeare family is granted a coat of arms; Hamnet, Shakespeare's only son, dies and is buried on August 11.

1597
A second Spanish Armada is scattered by bad weather before it can reach England; Shakespeare purchases a home, New Place, in Stratford but fails to pay his taxes in London.

1598
Francis Meres praises Shakespeare's skill in *Palladis Tamia;* the Theatre in Shoreditch is torn down and transported to Bankside, where it is reconstructed and renamed the Globe.

1599
The Globe opens in Bankside; it becomes the theater commonly associated with the Lord Chamberlain's Men and the name of William Shakespeare.

1601
Essex attempts to overthrow Queen Elizabeth but fails and is executed; the earl of Southampton is imprisoned for his role in the revolt; John Shakespeare dies; the Lord Chamberlain's Men is investigated for its role in the failed rebellion.

1602
Shakespeare buys land and homes in Stratford; his right to possess a coat of arms is attacked.

1603
Queen Elizabeth dies, and King James of Scotland becomes the new ruler of England; after James assumes the throne, the Lord Chamberlain's Men is issued a royal license and changes its name to the King's Men in honor of its new patron; the plague ravages London, and public theaters are closed.

1604
Since Shakespeare is a member of the King's Men and, subsequently, a member of James's household, he is granted four yards of red cloth for a royal procession through London.

1605
The Gunpowder Plot to blow up the king and English Parliament is discovered and foiled; Shakespeare purchases a half-interest in tithes (profits from farms) in Old Stratford, Welcombe, and Bishopton.

1607
Captain John Smith establishes Jamestown in the colony of Virginia; Susanna, Shakespeare's oldest daughter, marries John Hall on June 5; Shakespeare's youngest brother, Edmund, dies in London and is buried on December 31.

1608
Elizabeth Hall, Shakespeare's first granddaughter, is baptized on February 21; Shakespeare's mother, Mary, dies and is buried on September 9; Shakespeare sues John Addenbrooke for debt and becomes a one-seventh sharer in the new Blackfriars Theatre; the Blackfriars becomes the second, and more profitable, home for the King's Men.

1609
Shakespeare's *Sonnets* is published without authorization.

1610
Shakespeare begins semiretirement.

1611

The King James Bible is published; Shakespeare is in court with other citizens to defend his Stratford tithes; he writes *The Tempest,* his farewell play.

1612

Shakespeare is called as a witness in a lawsuit brought against Christopher Mountjoy by his son-in-law Stephen Belott about the terms of an arranged marriage to Mountjoy's daughter; Shakespeare's brother Gilbert dies and is buried on February 3.

1613

Shakespeare's only surviving brother, Richard, dies and is buried on February 4; in London, Shakespeare purchases the Blackfriars Gatehouse; he and Richard Burbage (his business partner) are each paid forty-four shillings for making an "impressa" (an emblem or motto).

1614

Shakespeare plays a small role in a lawsuit to oppose the enclosure of lands in Welcombe that would affect his tithes.

1616

Shakespeare's youngest daughter, Judith, marries Thomas Quiney; less than a month later, Quiney is summoned to court on fornication charges and a public scandal ensues; Shakespeare becomes ill with an unknown sickness; sensing that death is near, he revises his will and dies on April 23.

1623

A monument to Shakespeare is established in the Holy Trinity Church of Stratford; Shakespeare's wife, Anne, dies; the First Folio, a collection of nearly all of Shakespeare's plays, is first published in November.

Chronology of Shakespeare's Works

1589–1590
Henry VI, Part 1

1590–1591
Henry VI, Part 2
Henry VI, Part 3

1590–1593
Titus Andronicus
Sir Thomas More

1592–1593
Richard III
The Comedy of Errors
"Venus and Adonis"

1593–1594
"The Rape of Lucrece"
The Taming of the Shrew

1593–1595
Sonnets

1594
The Two Gentlemen of Verona

1594–1595
Love's Labor's Lost
King John

1595
Richard II

1595–1596
Romeo and Juliet
A Midsummer Night's Dream

1596–1597
The Merchant of Venice
Henry IV, Part 1

1597
The Merry Wives of Windsor

1598
Henry IV, Part 2

1598–1599
Much Ado About Nothing

1599
Henry V
Julius Caesar
As You Like It

1600–1601
Hamlet

1601
"The Phoenix and Turtle"
Twelfth Night

1601–1602
Troilus and Cressida

1602–1603
All's Well That Ends Well

1604
Measure for Measure
Othello

1605
King Lear

1606
Macbeth
Antony and Cleopatra

1607–1608
Coriolanus
Timon of Athens
Pericles

1609–1610
Cymbeline
The Winter's Tale

1611
The Tempest

1612
Henry VIII

1612–1613
Cardenio

1613
The Two Noble Kinsmen

Works Consulted

Editions of *Macbeth*

The Tragedy of Macbeth has been widely published over the last four centuries, and many different versions of the play are available. Students of Shakespeare should secure an annotated, unabridged, uncensored version of the play. Paperback versions that meet these criteria are available at most major bookstores.

G. Blakemore Evans, ed., *The Riverside Shakespeare*. Boston: Houghton Mifflin, 1974. This is the version favored by scholars, critics, and biographers. This anthology contains complete versions of Shakespeare's plays and poems, illustrations, records of Shakespeare's life, and introductory essays for each play and poem. *The Riverside Shakespeare* also contains criticism written by Shakespeare's contemporaries. It is the version that was used for compiling this book.

Biographies of William Shakespeare

Edmund Chambers, *A Short Life of Shakespeare with the Sources*, ed. Charles Williams. London: Oxford University Press, 1963. An excellent abridged version of Chambers's two-volume biography of William Shakespeare.

Dennis Kay, *William Shakespeare: His Life and Times*. New York: Twayne, 1995. Respected Renaissance scholar Dennis Kay examines Shakespeare's life and the world in which he lived.

A. L. Rowse, *Shakespeare the Man*. New York: St. Martin's, 1988. A. L. Rowse is a celebrated Elizabethan historian who has written extensively on Renaissance England and William Shakespeare. His biography is an excellent source for information on Shakespeare.

S. Schoenbaum, *William Shakespeare: A Compact Documentary Life*. New York: Oxford University Press, 1987. S. Schoenbaum is a professor of Renaissance studies at the University of Maryland and has written a couple of biographies of Shakespeare.

Katherine Baker Siepmann, ed., *Benet's Reader's Encyclopedia*. 3rd ed. New York: Harper and Row, 1987. This book provides the reader with everything from definitions of literary terms to author biographies to summaries of literary works.

Thomas Thrasher, *The Importance of William Shakespeare*. San Diego: Lucent Books, 1999. A biography of Shakespeare that includes illustrations and a chronology of his life and plays.

Historical Background

Stephanie Hanna, "Coincidence or Curse?" *British Heritage*, June/July 2000. This article explores the "curse" of *Macbeth*.

Bruce Heydt, "Fair and Foul Macbeth," *British Heritage*, June/July 2000. This article explores the differences between the historical Macbeth and Shakespeare's Macbeth.

William L. Lace, *Elizabethan England*. San Diego: Lucent Books, 1995. A history of the events of Elizabethan England.

Mr. William Shakespeare and the Internet (http://shakespeare.palomar. edu). This website contains the complete works of Shakespeare, a brief biography of the bard, some literary criticism, and links to other Shakespearean sites.

E. M. W. Tillyard, *The Elizabethan World Picture*. New York: Vintage Books, 1942. A brief account of the ideas that shaped the Elizabethan mind, including the Chain of Being.

Diane Yancey, *Life in the Elizabethan Theater*. San Diego: Lucent Books, 1997. This book explores what life would be like for a person who worked in the theater during Shakespeare's time.

Literary Criticism

M. H. Abrams, ed., *The Norton Anthology of English Literature*, vol. 1, 6th ed. New York: W. W. Norton, 1993. This exhaustive two-volume set is a basic university-level text covering a major portion of English literature. It contains select critical essays on Shakespeare and a good sampling of his works. *The Norton Anthology* contains annotations and a glossary.

Victor L. Cahn, *Shakespeare the Playwright*. New York: Greenwood, 1991. An easy-to-read book that offers guidance in understanding each of Shakespeare's plays.

Gareth Lloyd Evans, *The Upstart Crow: An Introduction to Shakespeare's Plays*. London: J. M. Dent and Sons, 1982. This book offers essays that explore each of Shakespeare's plays and directions for understanding them.

Levi Fox, *The Shakespeare Handbook*. Boston: G. K. Hall, 1987. An excellent book that provides summaries of Shakespeare's works.

Northrop Frye, *Northrop Frye on Shakespeare*. Ed. Robert Sandler. New Haven, CT: Yale University Press, 1986. An interesting and easy-to-read book in which the renowned literary critic Northrop Frye offers his views on several of Shakespeare's most famous plays.

F. E. Halliday, ed., *Shakespeare and His Critics*. New York: Schocken Books, 1963. This anthology contains more than three hundred years of critical commentary on Shakespeare and his plays and poems.

Alfred Harbage, ed., *Shakespeare: The Tragedies.* Englewood Cliffs, NJ: Prentice-Hall, 1964. This anthology offers critical comments on Shakespeare's tragedies by respected early twentieth-century critics.

Paul A. Jorgensen, *William Shakespeare: The Tragedies.* Boston: Twayne, 1985. Written by a respected Shakespeare scholar, this book scrutinizes several of Shakespeare's key plays in terms of themes, plots, characters, and symbols.

Peter Quennell and Hamish Johnson, *Who's Who in Shakespeare.* New York: Oxford University Press, 1995. This book provides a complete guide to the characters who appear in Shakespeare's plays.

Michael Baird Saenger, "Shakespeare's *Macbeth,*" *Explicator,* Spring 1995. This interesting article explores the similarities between Shakespeare's *Macbeth* and Christopher Marlowe's *Doctor Faustus.*

Stanley Wells, *A Dictionary of Shakespeare.* New York: Oxford University Press, 1998. This concise dictionary of "all things Shakespeare" contains alphabetically arranged entries guiding the reader to a wealth of information on all aspects of Shakespeare.

Index

PICTURE CREDITS

ABOUT THE AUTHOR

Thomas Thrasher lives in Long Beach with his cat, Jinx, and a 1965 Falcon. He teaches at Rio Hondo College in Whittier and at California State University, Long Beach. He also likes to dabble in poetry and fiction.